icons

G000036946

Mary Jo Martin, RSHM

Anne White

Ann Brook

Paul Gray

Yvonne May

Damian Walmsley

LIVING
a national project
of catechesis &
religious education
Catholic Bishops' Conference
of England & Wales
Sharing
OUR FAITH

Published by HarperCollins*Publishers* Ltd
77–85 Fulham Palace Road
London W6 8JB

© Department for Catholic Education and Formation, Bishops' Conference
of England and Wales

www.**Collins**Educational.com
On-line support for schools and colleges

First published 2001

ISBN 0 00 322131 8

Nihil Obstat Fr Anton Cowan, *censor*

Imprimatur Mgr Thomas Egan, V.G.
Westminster, 29th June 2000

The Nihil obstat and Imprimatur are a declaration that a book or pamphlet is
considered to be free from doctrinal or moral error. It has not implied that
those who have granted the Nihil obstat and imprimatur agree with the
contents, opinions or statements expressed.

British Library Cataloguing in Publication Data
A catalogue record for this book is available from the British Library

Project management by Terry Vittachi

Picture research by Kathy Lockley

Design and layout by Ken Vail Graphic Design, Cambridge

Cover design by Ken Vail Graphic Design, Cambridge

Cover photograph
1 The Bridgeman Art Library
2 Getty Images

Printed and bound by Scotprint, Haddington, Scotland

Illustrations
David Atkinson, pp. 17, 18, 19; Chris Coady, pp. 53, 54, 88, 90; Rosamund
Fowler, pp. 6, 20, 32, 83, 84, 85, 96; Stewart Lees, pp. 40, 41; Terry Riley,
pp. 8, 9, 61, 95; Lee Sullivan, pp. 12, 13, 33, 38, 39, 44, 46, 52, 56, 59, 60,
77, 94; Curtis Tappenden, p. 46; Mike Taylor, pp. 8, 9, 10, 11.

Photographs
A & B News, monthly paper of the Diocese of Arundel & Brighton, p. 29;
AKG London, pp. 24, 25, 42, 63, 79/Erich Lessing, p. 66; Ancient Art &
Architecture Collection, pp. 9, 17, 19; Andes Press Agency/© Alain Pinoges,
p. 37/Carlos Reyes, pp. 29, 64, 65, 68, 74, 92; Art Directors & TRIP Photo
Library, pp. 30, 75/A Tovy, p. 91/Gibbs, pp. 17, 70/B Turner, p. 75/C Ryan,
p. 76/E James, p. 70/Helene Rogers, pp. 16, 18, 22, 23, 26, 30, 36, 39, 42,
48, 51, 55, 58, 60, 65, 70, 71, 75, 78, 83, 86/J Hall, p. 18/J Okwesa, pp. 22,
26, 82/J Ringland, p. 63/J Highet, p. 28/Muzlish, p. 71/P Rauter, p. 26/S
Grant, p. 28/Steve Brock, p. 76/Viestii Collection, p. 28; Courtesy of the
Society of the Atonement, Graymoor, p. 68; Bridgeman Art Library
London/Private Collection p. 21; © CAFOD/Annie Bungeroth, p. 63/©
Matthew Carter, p. 26; © CORBIS/Bettmann, p. 67; Mary Evans Picture
Library, p. 79; Food Features, p. 23; Robert Harding Picture Library, pp. 7, 19,
30, 39, 78, 80; © HarperCollins Publishers, pp. 9, 10, 11, 35, 76; HCPT,
The Pilgrimage Trust, p. 50; Hulton Getty, p. 16; © Michael McCurdy, The
Man Who Planted Trees by Jean Giorno, Peter Owen Ltd, London, p. 81;
© The National Gallery, London, p. 49; provided by Archbishop Nichols,
p. 18; Courtesy One World Week, p. 55; PA Photos, p. 49; Pontifical Mission
Society, p. 26; Rex Features, pp. 23, 28, 39, 92/Seamus Murphy, p. 45/SIPA,
pp. 27, 87, 94; Science Photo Library Ltd p. 76; © SPG 1948, artist: Alfred
Thomas, p.7; Still Pictures/Dominque Halleux, p. 80 TL/Julio Etchart, p. 82;
© USPG Archives, p. 7; all rights reserved, Vie de Jesus, MAFA, 27 rue du
Marechal Joffre, F-78000, Versailles, p. 7; John Walmsley Photo Library,
p. 80; © The Dean & Chapter of Westminster, p. 94; Wiener Library, p. 79.

Text
The publishers gratefully acknowledge the following for permission to
reproduce copyright material. Every effort has been made to contact the
holders of copyright material, but if any have been inadvertently
overlooked, the publishers will be pleased to make the necessary
arrangements at the first opportunity.

p. 23, extract from *The Letters of J R R Tolkien* by Humphrey Carpenter
and Christopher Tolkien, published by HarperCollins Publishers; p. 32,
excerpts from the English translation of 'Rite of Baptism for Children'
© 1969, International Committee on English in the Liturgy Inc, (ICEL); all
rights reserved; reprinted with permission; p. 37, Extract from 'God Beyond
All Names', © 1990 Bernadette Farrell, published by OCP Publications,
5536 NE Hassalo, Portland, OR 97213; all rights reserved; used with
permission; p. 38, extract from 'Your Words Are Spirit And Life', © 1993
Bernadette Farrell, published by OCP Publications, 5536 NE Hassalo,
Portland, OR 97213; all rights reserved; used with permission; p. 56,
extract from 'Jesus, Lamb of God', ©1982, 1989 Paul Inwood, published
by OCP Publications, 5536 NE Hassalo, Portland, OR 97213; all rights
reserved; used with permission; p. 60, The English translation of the
Confiteor ('I Confess') and the Absolution ('May Almighty God') from *The
Roman Missal*, © 1973, International Committee on English in the Liturgy,
Inc; all rights reserved; reprinted with permission; p. 62, 'Look around you,
can you see', Jodi Page Clark, *Kyrie Eleison*, © 1976
Celebration/Kingsway's Thankyou Music, PO Box 75, Eastbourne, East
Sussex BN23 6NW, UK; used with permission; pp. 72–3, extract from *A
Passover Haggadah and the Central Conference of American Rabbis*
edited by Herbert Bronstein, © 1974, 1975, 1982 by The Central
Conference of American Rabbis; used by permission of Viking Penguin, a
division of Penguin Putnam Inc; p. 79, extract from *The Cost of
Discipleship* by Dietrich Bonhoeffer, published by SCM Press, reprinted
with permission; p. 80, extract from 'Unless A Grain Of Wheat', © 1983
Bernadette Farrell, published by OCP Publications, 5536 NE Hassalo,
Portland, OR 97213; all rights reserved; used with permission; p. 85,
extracts from *Meditations with Julian of Norwich*, introduction and versions
by Brendan Doyle, published by Bear & Company, Rochester VT 05767,
© 1983 Bear & Company Inc; reprinted with permission; p. 87, extract from
Strength to Love by Martin Luther King Jr, published by Hodder &
Stoughton Limited; reprinted with permission of Laurence Pollinger Limited
and the Estate of Martin Luther King; p. 91, extract from 'Only A Shadow'
© 1971, Carey Landry and North American Liturgy Resources (NALR),
5536 NE Hassalo, Portland, OR 97213; all rights reserved; used with
permission; 'Christ looked at the People' by Caryll Houselander, from
Flowering Tree published by Sheed & Ward, 1945, reprinted with
permission of the publishers.

p. 55: One World Week enables people to learn about global issues, and
take action for global justice. They provide Action Resources, including a
kit for use in schools. Contact One World Week for more information:
enquiries@oneworldweek.org

Scriptures quoted from The Good News Bible published by the Bible
Societies/HarperCollins Publishers limited, UK, © American Bible Society,
1966, 1971, 1976, 1992.

Foreword

On behalf of the Bishops' Conference, I am very pleased to welcome the publication of *Icons*.

Diocesan RE advisers, teachers and many others from all the dioceses of England and Wales have worked extremely hard in the production of this programme, which forms an important part of the National Project. I thank them for their dedication and perseverance.

At the Low Week 2000 Meeting of the Bishops' Conference of England and Wales, the bishops published a statement on Religious Education in Catholic Schools. In it they said that the primary purpose of classroom religious education in a Catholic school is:

'To draw pupils into a systematic study of the teaching of the Church, the saving mystery of Christ which the Church proclaims.' (para 7)

In undertaking this task, schools will benefit greatly from the provision of good teaching resources. For this reason I welcome *Icons*, for it will help Catholic schools to fulfil these expectations during the critical years of Key Stage Three.

In their statement, the bishops also stated:

'The importance of the teacher of RE cannot be exaggerated. We are most grateful to all those teachers who, week in and week out, have contributed to the religious education of pupils in our schools ... We salute the generosity of the teachers who have brought not only a love of their faith to their teaching but also a deep concern for the well-being of every pupil.' (para 12)

I gladly repeat that thanks and express my own encouragement for teachers in their important task.

Archbishop Vincent Nichols
Chairman
Department for Catholic Education and Formation

6 June 2000

Acknowledgements

Icons is the fruit of a shared vision, commitment and work. It derives its strength from a long and rigorous process of consultation with Bishops, Diocesan RE advisers, teachers and students of all twenty-two dioceses of England and Wales. It is a key component of the Bishops' national project of catechesis and religious education.

Thanks, first of all, to Bishop Edwin Regan, Chairman of the Steering Committee of the National Project, for his leadership and commitment, and the members of that Committee: Mr Anthony Clark, Canon Peter Humfrey, Sr Victoria Hummell, Rev Liam Kelly, Mrs Oona Stannard and Rev George Stokes.

Thanks to the Bishops' Conference, and in particular to Archbishops Patrick Kelly and Vincent Nichols, Bishops Daniel Mullins, Edwin Regan and Peter Smith for their time and attention in the final stages of scrutiny.

Since 1996, Diocesan secondary RE advisers and teacher representatives have been actively involved in the development of *Icons*. For their time, energy and expertise, thanks to: Rev Joseph Quigley, Miss Collette Dawson, Rev Ieuan Wyn Jones, Rev Dennis Sutton, Miss Marjorie Parker, Rev Sean Hall, Miss Anne Sales, Miss Sheila O'Brien, Mr Nicholas Weeks, Rev Nigel Bavidge, Rev Des Seddon, Mr Tony Lamb, Sr Aidan Richards, Sr Margaret Horan, Ms Anne-Marie McIntosh, Sr Maura McMenamin, Mr Adrian Dempsey, Mrs Rita Price, Br Charles Gay, Mr Paul Uden, Mr Paul Rowlands, Rev Adrian Morrin, Sr Dolores Lynn, and Ms Noreen O'Neill, secondary advisor of CAFOD. Thanks also to the teachers and students of the schools in every diocese who took part in the monitored trial in 1999 for their support. We hope they will recognise some of their ideas in the final text.

Particular thanks to those who were involved in the early stages of development: Mr Tony Castle, Mrs Jane Ranzetta, Mr Simon Danes and to their families and schools: St Bernard's School, Westcliff on Sea, New Hall School, Chelmsford and Cardinal Newman, Hove. Also to Maria Ivko, whose creative contribution remains as a lasting memorial to her dedication to Catholic education. May she rest in peace.

Special thanks to Dr Thomas Allain-Chapman, Commissioning Editor at HarperCollins, with whom the professional aspects of the work became a sharing of ideas that enhanced the development of *Icons*.

To Sisters Mary, Elizabeth and Cecelia and the staff at the Kairos Centre for their hospitality, interest and encouragement and care for our well-being during long working sessions.

To our families and friends we owe tremendous gratitude. They, too, laboured with us through their understanding, patience and listening. Special thanks to Sr Mary Jo's community of the Religious of the Sacred Heart of Mary, and colleagues at St Mary's College, Strawberry Hill, to Anne's colleagues at the Catholic Education Service and to the headteachers, staff and students of St Angela's, Forest Gate, St Bede's, Scunthorpe, St Benedict's, Whitehaven, St Bonaventure's, Forest Gate and St Mary's College, Hull. We could not have completed the task without your support.

Finally, thanks to all those involved in the final stages of production: text editor, picture research, designers, artists and photographers.

The journey has been long. In one sense, with the publication of the text, it has just begun. It has been a tremendous privilege to be part of the creation and development of *Icons*. Our hope is that teachers and students will find here a programme of religious education that enables, illumines and leads to a discovery of the power of faith and the adventure that is the search for meaning and for God.

Mary Jo Martin RSHM, Anne White, Ann Brook, Paul Gray, Yvonne May, Damian Walmsley

Contents

1A In a time and a place

In this section of our work we will be learning:

- about the importance of a person's cultural, social and religious background
- about Jesus, a Jew of the first century, the Son of God.

Start where you are

Do a survey of the class. How many different family backgrounds are represented? For example: a French great-grandmother, an Irish father, Yorkshire cousins, and a Scottish aunt.

Make a list of any family customs or traditions that you think may have come from these different cultures. For example, New Year celebrations are special in Scotland.

In a small group, share your findings.

Collect and display your findings using some of the following headings to help you: Religion, Country, Language, Customs, Dress, Food.

These things make up your family background. Within your family people also have different tastes in music and fashion. These influence your lifestyle. They influence the way you see yourself and the way others see you. This diversity can make life rich and interesting. It can also lead to misunderstandings and problems.

Research cultural diversity among your family and friends in music or fashion.

Write a report using words and pictures. Show how people's lifestyles are influenced by their tastes.

Discuss

What do you think we gain by this diversity? What would we lose without it?

Extension

- Find a way to share your findings with the rest of the year group.

Pause for thought

*To understand me **you** need to know …*
*What do **I** need to know to understand you?*

Words we use

diversity – number or variety of anything; for example, nationalities in a school; range of differences; for example, in dress styles or tastes in music

culture – way of life, values, attitudes of a particular group of people; for example, Western culture, pop culture, youth culture

to cultivate – to work with; for example, the earth, agriculture
– to work at a particular style, skill or aptitude; for example, hairstyle, knowledge of folk music, an accent or style of speaking

Jesus the Jew

To understand Jesus it is essential to know the historical background and culture of the country where he was born and lived.

The Gospels of Matthew, Mark, Luke and John do not record what Jesus looked like. Why not?
What is your image of Jesus?
Where does it come from?

Although we have no portrait of Jesus, it is almost certain that he would have had the typical features and colouring of a man born in the Middle East 2,000 years ago.

The language that he spoke, the food he ate and the clothes that he wore were part of the culture of the day.
In spite of this, artists have imagined Jesus as being like them and used their own countries as the background for their portraits of him.

An Israeli man.

The Last Supper, artist unknown.

Christ entering Jerusalem on Palm Sunday, artist unknown, 1938.

Calming the Storm, Alfred Thomas, 1948.

Think and talk

Which country do you think each of these represents?
Why do people want to show Jesus in ways familiar to themselves?
What is each artist trying to say about Jesus?

Write a short commentary for each picture (not more than 20 words) which begins: 'This artist presents Jesus as ...'

Check your learning

What do you think are the three most important things someone should know about Jesus' historical background?

Jesus' life in Palestine

Jesus was born in Bethlehem, in Palestine, sometime around 6–4BC. He lived his life as a faithful Jew. He worshipped as a Jew and obeyed the Law. He was a loving son and grew up in a village community. In the synagogue he learned the Torah.

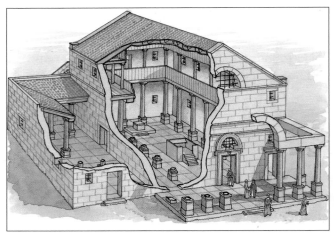

The synagogue: a place for prayer and meeting.

The Synagogue

In every town there was a synagogue. It was a house of worship, a meeting hall, a courtroom and a school. On the Sabbath day people would meet for prayer and teaching. The scrolls of the Hebrew Scriptures were kept in an Ark. They were treated with great reverence because this was God's word for his people. The rabbi, teacher, taught the boys to read and recite the Torah.

The Ark was a reminder of the carved chest in which the tablets of the Law were housed on the Israelites' journey through the desert.

Torah is Hebrew for 'teaching' or 'guidance'. The Torah consists of five books: Genesis, Exodus, Leviticus, Numbers and Deuteronomy. It is the first part of the Hebrew Bible. It is the law given by Moses to show God's people how they should live.

Scrolls were made of parchment and hand-written.

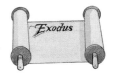

The second part of the Hebrew Bible is called the Prophets, which in Hebrew is *Nev'im*. It includes historical writings, for example, Samuel and Kings; and prophetic writings, for example, Isaiah, Jeremiah, Ezekiel and the twelve minor prophets.

The third part of the Hebrew Bible is the Writings, which in Hebrew is *Ketuvim*. It includes Psalms, Proverbs, Esther, Ecclesiastes, Daniel, Chronicles, Ruth and the love poetry of the Song of Songs.

If you take T (Torah), N (Nev'im) and K (Ketuvim) you get TNK. Add vowels and you get Tanakh, the Hebrew word for Bible.

In synagogue services the scrolls were carried from the Ark where they were kept. The synagogue leader could ask any man of the community to read the appointed Scripture.

נביאים
Nevi'im

כתובים
Ketuvim

A mosaic floor of a sixth century synagogue in Bethlehem.

Think and talk

Luke's gospel tells of Jesus being asked to read. Read Luke 4:14–22. What do you think the people in the synagogue thought?

Note: Jews speak of the Hebrew Scriptures. Christians call these writings the Old Testament. The order of books in the Hebrew and Christian Scriptures are different.

Extension

* Create your own Wordsearch using the following:
  Synagogue, Sabbath, Torah, Ark, rabbi, Hebrew, Exodus, Psalms, scrolls.
* Remember, words can go backwards, diagonally and vertically.
* Try not to make it too easy. Exchange your Wordsearch with a partner. Compare notes.

The shofar, a ram's horn, used for the call to prayer.

1A In a time and a place

The Temple

The Temple in Jesus' time was a very large and beautiful building. King Herod had built it in place of King Solomon's temple, which had been destroyed by the Babylonians. The Jewish Council, the Sanhedrin, met there. The Sanhedrin controlled religious matters and acted as a criminal court. It was made up of Sadducees, Pharisees and Scribes. The leader of the Sanhedrin was the High Priest.

It was in the Temple in Jerusalem, not the local synagogue, that sacrifice was offered. Only priests could enter the holiest part of the Temple and only the High Priest could enter the holy of holies, the most sacred area of all.

The High Priest.

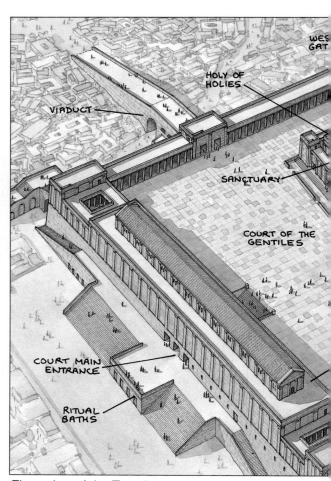

Floor plan of the Temple.

The Outer Court: the Court of the Gentiles

Gentiles, non-Jews, were not allowed beyond this court. Traders could be found here selling birds and animals to be used for sacrifices. It was also a place to change Roman money into Temple money.

The Court of the Women

Women and children were not allowed to go beyond this area. It was a favourite meeting place for families when they came to Jerusalem on pilgrimage.

The Court of the Israelites

Only Jewish men were allowed to enter here. They could see the altar of sacrifice and the offerings being made to God. At the time of Jesus, animal sacrifices were an important part of Temple worship.

The Temple.

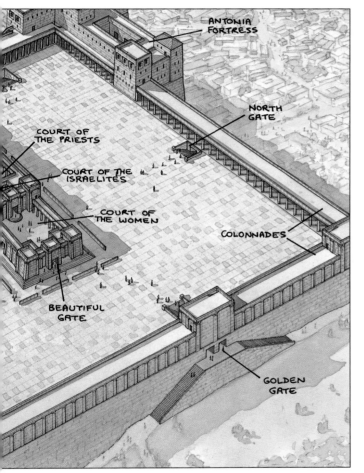

ANTONIA FORTRESS

NORTH GATE

COURT OF THE PRIESTS

COURT OF THE ISRAELITES

COURT OF THE WOMEN

COLONNADES

BEAUTIFUL GATE

GOLDEN GATE

The Court of Priests

This was exclusively reserved for priests. In this area was the altar on which the birds and animals were sacrificed. Only domestic animals could be sacrificed. This included pigeons and doves, the offerings of poor people.

The Holy of Holies

This was the innermost and most sacred part of the Temple. A large veil covered its entrance. Only the High Priest was allowed to enter, and he only went in once a year, on the Day of Atonement, Yom Kippur. He offered sacrifices and asked God's forgiveness in the name of all the people. On this day only he spoke aloud, in full, the name of God. This day marked a new start, a renewal of faithfulness to the laws of God.

Work in groups

- Read Luke 1:8–23 and Luke 2:22–38.
- Using the Temple outline to help you, write a step-by-step description of where the people in the stories would have gone in the Temple area, and what they would have seen.

1A In a time and a place

Politics at the time of Jesus

Jesus was born and brought up in an occupied land. Palestine was part of the Roman Empire. When Jesus was born, Herod the Great was king. He ruled the whole of Palestine, but when he died the territory was split between three of his sons. The Roman Emperor refused to give them the title of king, and eventually he replaced Archaeleus, ruler of the southern province, with a Roman governor. When Jesus began his mission this governor was Pontius Pilate. (Read Luke 3:1–3.) The Romans allowed the Jews to practise their own religion and so the Jews had their own religious authorities based in Jerusalem. The main Council was the Sanhedrin. This Council decided religious matters and acted as a law court. It could punish people who broke the religious law, but could not put a person to death.

Spotlight on the religious groups

Pharisees

They were the strictest in keeping the Law. The name means 'separated one'. They would have nothing to do with Gentiles or sinners. They not only tried to keep every part of the Torah, they studied it and added new interpretations. They usually took a leading part in running the synagogues.

Sadducees

They were a small, powerful and influential group. They were often the wealthy, upper-class Jews, conservative in matters of religion. Unlike the Pharisees, they accepted only the Torah and refused to accept new interpretations of the Law. Many of the Sadducees held powerful positions in the Sanhedrin. They were friendly towards the Romans in order to keep their position, and so were mistrusted by other Jews.

Scribes

They were also known as doctors of the Law, rabbis or lawyers. The Scribes became teachers of Judaism and interpreted the Law for people. Many of the Scribes were Pharisees.

Zealots

They were nationalists and hated the Roman conquerors. They were waiting for the Messiah to lead them in battle against the Romans. They wanted to set up God's Kingdom, and to do this they were willing to put up armed resistance against the Romans. To the Romans they were terrorists, but many Jews saw them as freedom fighters.

Think and talk

1. The Jews had to pay taxes to the Romans. How do you think a Sadducee and a Zealot would feel about paying taxes to the Romans? Why?

2. What do you think each group hoped to get from the Messiah? Why might each of these religious groups have expected Jesus to join them?

Extension

Essenes

Most of them lived in the desert where they followed a strict religious life, like the monks of later times. They were even stricter than the Pharisees and tried to keep the Jewish religion pure. They believed that they alone were the true people of God. A collection of scrolls was found in the desert at Qumran, north of the Dead Sea, in 1948. These are probably part of their library.

Research: find out about the Dead Sea Scrolls.

1A In a time and a place

In the footsteps of Jesus

Jesus probably never travelled more than 200 miles from the place where he was born. For the first 30 years of his life he probably lived at home and worked in the family business of carpentry. It was only during the last three years of his life that he began travelling around Palestine preaching and teaching. He was about 30 when he began his mission. He travelled around from town to town and village to village, bringing the Good News to everyone he met.

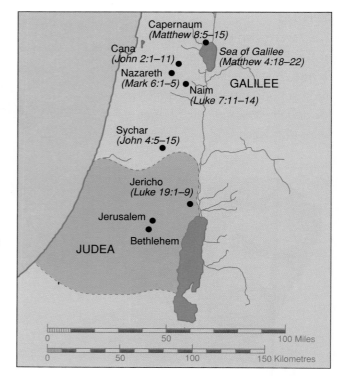

Look at the map

1. Find out whom Jesus met at each of these places.
2. How was meeting Jesus good news for them?
3. Plan a five-day itinerary for pilgrims wanting to visit important places in the life of Jesus. Start at Bethlehem and finish at Jerusalem. Suggest which places they should visit in between. Explain why each place is important in the life of Jesus.

Use your geography skills and a present-day map to work out distances. Plan the journeys so that you make the best use of time. Use as sources either a guidebook or travel brochures.

Pause for thought

I was glad when they said to me, "Let us go to the Lord's house". (Psalm 122:1)

Homework 🏛

Pilgrims' map: *Copymaster* 1

Use the outline to make a map for your pilgrims. Mark Bethlehem 'Day 1' and Jerusalem 'Day 5'.

Classwork ✍

People will often become members of a faith community through their families.
Jesus learned the prayers and beliefs of the Jewish faith from Mary and Joseph and the Jewish community of Nazareth.

A. *Read the following: Psalm 84; Psalm 23; Psalm 63; Psalm 119:145–152; and Psalm 89. Jesus would have prayed these psalms. In groups identify:*
  ◆ *what each one says about God*
  ◆ *when you think Jesus might have used these prayers.*

B. *Read Matthew 4:1–11 and Deuteronomy 8:3; 6:16–18; and 6:13. What do these passages tell us about how Jesus knew and loved the Scriptures? How did this help him to deal with temptation?*
Make notes of your findings.

C. *Read Mark 11:15–19; Isaiah 56:7; and Jeremiah 7:11. What were people doing that made Jesus so angry? What was wrong with what they were doing? Explain what Jesus is saying about God and about the Temple.*

Links

Pause for thought

Christians should never forget that Jesus was a Jew.

Test ?

1. What caused tension between the Jews and the Romans?
2. Explain the importance of the Sanhedrin.
3. What is the Torah?
4. Why was the synagogue important?
5. Why was the Temple important?

Another step

Read Matthew 5:1–17. Use the passage to explain Matthew's message that Jesus calls people to go beyond 'the letter of the Law' (verse 17, 'to make the teachings come true').

Faith alive

The *Shema* is the prayer at the heart of Jewish faith.
(Deuteronomy 6:4–9)
It affirms belief in One God.

Key *words*

In your personal file write down the following words and a one-sentence explanation for each:

Gentile

Pharisee

Sadducee

Torah

Zealot

Challenge
No one has made more difference to the world than Jesus has.

Hebrew Scriptures

Hear, O Israel, the Lord is our God, the Lord is One.

Blessed be the name of his glorious majesty for ever and ever.

You shall love the Lord your God with all your heart, and with all your soul, and with all your might. And these words which I command you today shall be in your heart.

Christian Old Testament

Hear, O Israel: the Lord our God is one Lord; and you shall love the Lord your God with all your heart, and with all your soul, and with all your might. And these words which I command you this day shall be upon your heart.

1B Making history

Family history

It all began with a cancelled flight! My mum, only she wasn't my mum then, was very disappointed when her holiday flight to Florida was cancelled because of a hurricane. It was raining at Manchester too, so she decided to go for a coffee. The only spare seat in the cafe was at a table where a young man was sitting. He was looking fed up. They got talking and you could say that it was lucky for me that they did. It turned out that he had also been going to Florida. It turned out that they went together on their honeymoon. It turned out that they had me!

A family today.

An Edwardian family.

Think of events in your own life or in the life of your family that had a big impact.

Either	*or*
write your own story that begins 'It all began …' or 'If I hadn't …'	collect one or two stories from a member of your family or a family friend about important events in your family history. Record them in words, pictures or multi-media. Include their reasons and your own for choosing these stories.

A nation, like a family, has a story: its history.

Brainstorm a VIP list for England or Wales in your lifetime.

Who are the men and women who have made a difference to the nations' stories?

Work as a class

Make a list of reasons for choosing VIPs under two headings:
On the list because …
Off the list because …

Extension

'You only know where you are going if you know where you have come from.'
Discuss what this says about the importance of history (for a family or country).

Pause for thought

People who do not know their own history are destined to repeat it.

Check your learning

What do the following acronyms stand for?
BC   AD   BCE   CE

Put the following in order:
Victorians   Anglo-Saxons   dinosaurs
Romans   Tudors

The Church in Britain

In this section of work you will be studying the first 1,500 years of Christianity in Britain. The outline of key people and events will give you ideas for your own projects.

Pre-history

Joseph of Arimathea. The Holy Grail.

The Glastonbury thorn.

Roman Britain (AD 50–450)

Among the Roman settlers and soldiers were Christians. There is also evidence that Christian Britons had links with the Church in Gaul and Rome. Missionaries from Britain carried the gospel to Ireland and to the northern tribes of Picts and Scots.

York
Eboracum

Colchester
Camulodunum

Newport
Caerleon

St. Albans
Verulanium

London
Londinium

Dover
Dubris

The first martyrs of England and Wales: Alban, Julius and Aaron.

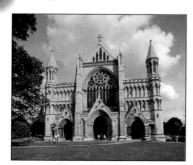

The cathedral marks the place of Alban's martydrom about AD 286.

After the Romans left Britain the Anglo-Saxon tribes spread through the country. They lived in tribal groups and the spread of Christianity depended on the good will of the leader or king.

Anglo Saxon Britain (AD 450–1066)

Whitby Abbey today.

Bede's tomb in Durham Cathedral.

Some key dates

565	Cuthbert founds the monastery on Iona.
596	Pope Gregory sends Augustine to England.
597	Augustine welcomed by King Ethelbert and Queen Bertha.
635	King Oswald invites Aidan to Northumbria.
664	At the Synod of Whitby the Church in England agrees to follow the Roman custom for fixing the date of Easter.
731	Bede completes his *Ecclesiatical History of the English People*.
793	Lindisfarne destroyed by Viking raiders.
794	Jarrow with its library is burned.
871	Alfred becomes King of Wessex. After winning peace with the Danes, he encourages education and a revival of building.
960	Dunstan becomes Archbishop of Canterbury.
1042	Edward the Confessor becomes King.

Some key people

Bede, born circa 672—673. Aged seven, sent to the monastery at Wearmouth to be educated. Became a monk and spent most of his life in Jarrow. He was a writer and teacher.

Gildas, born circa 500 in Wales. Became a monk and is best known as the author of *The Devastation of Britain*.

Pope Gregory, born circa 540 to a noble Roman family. As Prefect of Rome he was responsible for the city's finance, its buildings and food supplies. Became a monk in 574. In 585 he was elected abbot of his monastery, and in 590 became Pope.

Christianity was a light in the 'Dark Ages'. Missionary saints built up Christian communities. Devotion to St Peter was strong and pilgrims journeyed to his tomb. Strong links developed between the Church in Britain and Rome. Archbishops went to Rome to receive the pallium from the Pope. It was a symbol of their authority and unity with the successor of St Peter. In the twenty-first century this still continues.

Archbisho still receiv the palliun from the Pope.

Medieval Britain (1066–1500)

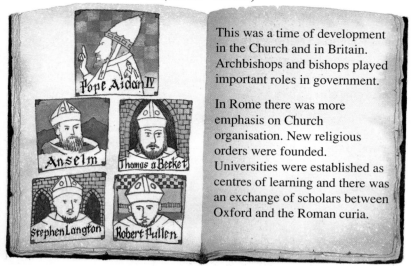

This was a time of development in the Church and in Britain. Archbishops and bishops played important roles in government.

In Rome there was more emphasis on Church organisation. New religious orders were founded. Universities were established as centres of learning and there was an exchange of scholars between Oxford and the Roman curia.

Canterbury Cathedral.

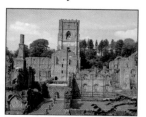

Fountains Abbey, founded 1132 by Cistercian monks.

The Church was powerful. Bishops were advisers to the kings and acted as judges. Some became political figures rather than pastors. The Church also had its own law courts. These situations sometimes led to tension.

Bishops and monasteries owned large estates and collected tithes, taxes in money and goods. Religious orders provided the only care for the sick and poor. Monasteries played an important part in education and the economy. For example, some were the largest landholders and farmers in an area. Abbeys farmed the land producing food, sheep and wool. They offered hospitality, worship, prayer and education.

Peterhouse, Cambridge.

The universities became centres for learning, but the division between clerics and lay people was great. Geoffrey Chaucer's *Canterbury Tales* tells of a group of pilgrims on their way to Becket's shrine at Canterbury. It gives an interesting cross-section of the men and women of the time.

Pilgrimages were a popular devotion, and shrines like those of Thomas at Canterbury, Cuthbert at Durham and Winifrid at Holywell received many offerings.

Changes

In Rome a system of Church management developed. It became known as the *Curia*, a kind of 'civil service' to organise the Church's business. Records show that many English scholars found employment in the Curia. Alongside the many positive developments there was unrest. In Britain and in Europe countries began to build up their national power. People began to see education and skills as personal goals. England and France fought a series of wars. English, Welsh, Scots and Irish struggled for power. There was a succession of rival popes supported by the kings and princes of England, France and Germany when they thought it would be to their advantage.

Village life

Village life centred on the parish church.

Everyone in the village would have a hand in building the church. Often a rich nobleman or merchant would provide the money; some of the huge parish churches of East Anglia are evidence of this. Rich families would set aside money for priests to say Masses for them. The priests were called chantry priests and some churches had special chantry chapels.

In church people prayed and learned their faith. Mass was said in Latin. Those who had been educated at monastery schools would understand it, but some parish priests only knew enough Latin to say Mass and most lay people did not understand it. There was no homily; instead people would gather when a travelling preacher arrived. The best-known preaching orders were the Franciscans and Dominicans. Most people could not read, so stained glass windows, statues and wall mosaics became their Bible.

Feast days were holidays and many had special customs. Sometimes this was a fair. Stalls were set up selling farm produce and crafts, food and drink. Travelling jugglers, acrobats and actors entertained people.

Plays were a way of hearing the stories of the Bible. In some larger towns these 'miracle' or 'mystery' plays were great productions. Everyone took part. The guilds, companies of craftsmen, would take responsibility for one play. For example, at York the shipwrights took on the story of Noah building the ark, and at Coventry the fishers and mariners put on the story of the flood.

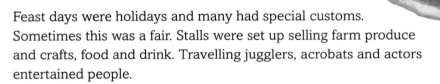

Homework

1. *Choose something from this section for individual projects. For example, one aspect of Church life in general – churches, stained glass windows, mystery plays, fairs – or a key person or event. You could focus on your local area. Remember that names – of villages, towns, churches, streets – can be clues.*

2. *Plan your project to include a handout or display that you can share with the rest of the class.*

3. *Display and share your work.*

Classwork

A. *Choose five new facts you have learned from this section of work. Explain your choice. Did anything surprise you or have special interest for you?*

B. *Write a short news item for a school or local newspaper titled 'I bet you never knew ...'. Your aim is to interest your readers in some aspect of local (or national) Church history.*

C. *Using evidence from the class project work, give reasons for and against learning Church history in school.*

Pause for thought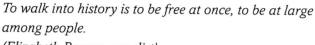

To walk into history is to be free at once, to be at large among people.
(Elizabeth Bowen, novelist)

Test ?

1. Give two reasons why history is important for (a) a family, (b) the Church.

2. Name one principal source book about the beginnings of the Church in Britain.

3. Why was the Synod of Whitby important for the Church in Britain?

4. Give as many reasons as you can to explain the importance of the monasteries for the development of the Church in Britain.

5. Give two reasons for tension between the Church and the State (king, non-clerics).

Key words

In your personal file write down the following words and a one-sentence explanation for each:

history

tradition

story

legend

Challenge
Our chief interest in the past is as a guide to the future. Why is the past important for the future?

Faith alive

A parson, good and true and poor:
… but rich in holy thought and work,
And a learned man was this clerk.
Christ's gospel he did truly preach,
His people most devoutly teach;
Kind in word and faithful to his task,
When troubles came his patience none surpassed,
And this he proved many a time.
When tithes were due he did not press the poor,
But often gave them of his own small store;
For himself he needed very little.

Wide was his parish, the houses far asunder,
But he was not put off by rain or thunder,
At times of sickness and of grief, to call
On the remotest, whether great or small …

A better priest than he I doubt there is.
He taught the law of Christ and the apostles twelve,
But first he knew and followed it himself.

(From the Prologue to *The Canterbury Tales*, The Parish Priest)

Another step

Create a dialogue between Chaucer's parish priest and a parish priest today.

1C A sense of vocation

Work in groups

Look at the pictures.
What qualities do these people need for their jobs?
What talents will they need and have to develop?
Write a brief job description for each job.
Share your work with the class.

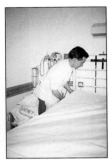

> **In this section of our work we will be learning:**
> ◆ what a vocation is
> ◆ some of the ways people respond to God's call.

Words we use

quality – a strength, way of behaving or attitude a person has; for example, he/she is always able to see the funny side of things

talent – a quality or gift a person has and works at or develops; for example, he/she has a real talent for music; he/she is clever with their hands; he/she has a talent for making people feel at ease

skill – an ability that a person develops in order to do a particular job; for example, he/she remembers people's names

gifted – having a quality, talent or skill that comes naturally

vocation – profession, job or trade someone follows; God's call in each person's life

A sense of self

Each person is gifted with a variety of talents. Often as we grow we become aware of them, or when we are asked to do a particular job.

Think of your talents. Remember to include 'inner' as well as 'outer', that is to say, outwardly visible talents.

Compare your answers with a partner.

Make a list of different ways these talents help you to contribute to the life of the groups you belong to: family, school, other; for example, team, club.

What or who has helped you to become aware of your personal qualities and talents?

Use your lists to make a class display of 'Talents for living'.

A person's qualities or talents often push them in the direction of a particular job or profession. This makes it essential to be honest about our strengths and weaknesses. Understanding ourselves and being open to situations are key to a true sense of self and personal vocation.

Words we use

self-esteem – a sense of personal value

self-knowledge – the ability to know your own strengths and weaknesses

self-confidence – the quality of being at ease and using your talents

As a class think of examples that show:
◆ what helps a person to grow in self-esteem
◆ when self-knowledge might be important
◆ what can undermine a person's self-confidence.

Who are you?

Some people find that their profession or job is a perfect way of expressing themselves. For others a job is a way of earning a living, and they find their sense of self and way of expressing themselves somewhere else. Some people, through no fault of their own, are unemployed. These facts encourage us to look beyond the profession or job. The answer to the question "Who are you?" has to be more than "I'm (unemployed, a bus driver, a writer)".

Pat lost her job when the local factory closed. So did a lot of other people in the town. Life was hard for a lot of families. Pat worried about her family and what they were going to do at Christmas. At the launderette she discovered that other people had the same worries. They shared them and tried to cheer up one another. One day someone thanked Pat. "What for?" she asked. "You're a good listener. You give people time to talk," was the answer. "Well, I've got plenty of time all right," she said, laughing. On the way home she thought, "It's more than that. I like listening because I like people."

Fred was a bus driver. Passengers warmed to his cheerful smile. He was a big man and there was something about the size of his great hands on the wheel that made people feel safe. Fred enjoyed his job, but his real sense of satisfaction came from something completely different. Among his family and friends he was known as the best cake decorator you could find. The great hands that looked so strong at the wheel of the bus could shape the most delicate flowers on a cake. The trellis and swirls of the decorations were amazing. His wife used to say, "It seems to come naturally to him. Just as well, because I'm all fingers and thumbs."

J R R Tolkien, the creator of imaginary worlds and their languages, told the story of when his interest in language began.
"I first tried to write a story when I was about seven. It was about a dragon. I remember nothing about it except a <u>philological</u> fact. My mother said nothing about the dragon, but pointed out that one could not say 'a green great dragon' but had to say 'a great green dragon'. I wondered why, and still do. The fact that I remember this is probably significant, as I do not think I ever tried to write a story again for many years, and was taken up with language." (Letter to W H Auden, 1955)

NB 'Philology' is the study of language. A philologist studies the history of languages.

What do the three people have in common?
What gives each one a sense of satisfaction?
How true would it be to say of each that he or she had 'found their vocation in life'?

Pause for thought

The tip of your finger is a constant reminder that 'I am unique'.

Check your learning ✓✓
Write one sentence to explain each of the following:
unique
Creator
'made in the image of God'.

Called by God

The Church believes that God creates each person. Each is unique. Each receives gifts and talents that they are called to use and develop all through life. Each is called to a unique relationship with God. Knowing this helps a person to have a true sense of self and a sense of vocation. A person's understanding about God is important in helping him or her to *discern* their vocation, and so is the advice of people she or he can trust.

to discern – to pray and reflect in order to make a choice that is true to God.

The Church believes that Jesus is unique in human history. He was truly God and knew the Father's plan for his life. He was truly human and had to grow in understanding of his vocation and make choices.

Study three gospel accounts about Jesus and his response to God's call. Work in a group.

One

Read Luke 2:41–52.

1. Why would the visit to the Temple be important for Jesus at the age of 12?
2. Why would Jesus be questioning the teachers of the Law?
3. Jesus' response to Mary and Joseph was "Why did you have to look for me? Didn't you know I had to be in my Father's house?"
   These are the first words spoken by Jesus in Luke's gospel. What is Luke's message about Jesus?

Jesus and the Scribes, Jusepe de Ribera, c 1625.

Two

Mark's gospel opens with crowds of people coming to be baptised by John, a wild-looking man from the desert. He stirs them up with a promise of someone greater than himself who will come and do great things for them. Then Jesus comes to the river where John was baptising. Read Mark 1:9–13.

1. How does Mark bring out the drama of this beginning?
2. What is Mark's message about Jesus?
3. Why was it important?
4. What did Jesus learn from his baptism?
5. What does this passage tell us about Jesus' mission from God his Father, his vocation?
6. What did Jesus do after he was baptised?
7. Why do you think he did this?
8. What shows that Jesus had to make a choice and that this was hard?

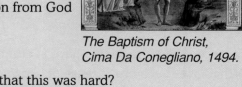

The Baptism of Christ, Cima Da Conegliano, 1494.

In groups, dramatise the passage you read. You may choose to improvise in role play, record a radio play with sound effects, or make a video.

How will you bring out the message that Jesus says "Yes" to his call from God his Father? How will you bring out the message that God the Holy Spirit is with Jesus?

Three

Mark's gospel does not give any details of how Jesus was tempted in the desert, but Luke's does. Jesus was alone so there were no witnesses. Luke is using the symbolic language of the Hebrew Scriptures to express what is important about Jesus and his mission.

Read Luke 4:1–14.

The Temptation of Christ, anon, c 1500.

Work in groups. Each group take one of the temptations.
1. What is Jesus offered?
2. What does he choose and why?
3. What is Luke's message about Jesus?
4. What is Luke's message about God?
5. What is Luke's message about human relationship with God?
6. What symbolic language does Luke use? How does it help the readers?

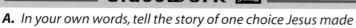

Classwork

A. In your own words, tell the story of one choice Jesus made and what helped him to make it.

B. Identify as many different choices made by Jesus as you can in the three Scripture passages you have studied. Choose two or three and explain what they say to you about Jesus and his mission.

C. "You are my Son, the Beloved, with you I am well pleased." How would knowing this have made a difference to Jesus?

Pause for thought

God sees beyond what we are to what we will be.

Mother of Jesus

The Church honours Mary for her unique vocation. Luke's gospel tells how God's messenger, the angel Gabriel, was sent to Mary of Nazareth to announce God's plan for her life. She was probably about 13 years old, the age when girls would be betrothed, that is to say, 'promised in marriage'.

Read Luke 1:26–38.

1. How does Luke show that God's call came as a surprise to Mary?
2. How did she feel?
3. What clues are there about the kind of person Mary was? As a class, look at the following qualities. Decide which helped Mary to say "Yes" to God.

open to God	selfishness	a sense of self
physical strength	hope	cleverness
trust	courage	confidence
good memory	health	ambition
patience	obedience	

4. What do you think makes Mary a role model for Christians of today?

Mary's heart was open to God before she conceived the Son of God.

1C A sense of vocation

Called to be ... What? How?

Look at the photographs.

Talk with a partner or in a group.
1. What is each called to be?
2. How does each follow that call?

World-wide mission

All Christians are called to proclaim the gospel. The Pontifical Mission Societies have a special care to support this vocation and encourage people to recognise that the Good News is for all people. The work is focused in four areas. David's story illustrates the work of the Society of St Peter the Apostle (SPA).

David Olemwanda is of the Masai people. He lives in Kenya. As a boy his favourite subject at school was science. During holidays and weekends he travelled long distances with the missionary priest. David would act as interpreter for the priest's work among the people in the villages, visiting the sick, listening to people's problems, serving Mass. He began to realise that his people needed their own Masai priest who understood their language and their way of life. When he spoke to his parents about this, they did not like the idea and so David did as they asked and went to university to study science. The call to become a priest did not go away, and at the end of his first year David's wish to study for the priesthood was fulfilled.

"The priest for the third millennium must have a concern for justice, an interest in youth and show that Christianity is African and not something foreign."

Research

Find out more about the SPA and its newsheet (*Mission Tomorrow*) and about:

- The Association for the Propagation of the Faith (APF)
- The Pontifical Missionary Union (PMU)
- Holy Childhood and Mission Together: 'Children helping Children'.

You may also like to research the work of the Mill Hill Missionary Society.

☰ Homework 🏛 ☰

Called to be ...

Write five tips for a Christian who is trying to discern God's call for her or him.

Links

Pause for thought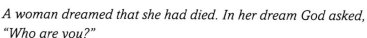

*A woman dreamed that she had died. In her dream God asked,
"Who are you?"*
"I'm the mayor's wife," she answered.
"Who are you?" God asked again.
"I'm the mother of four children," she said.
*"I didn't ask you whose wife or mother you are, but who you
are," God said.*
"I'm a Christian," she tried.
"I didn't ask you your religion," said God. "Who are you?"
"I'm a doctor," she said.
"I didn't ask you what your job was," said God. "Who are you?"
God's voice grew louder and louder and the woman woke up.
What do you think her dream was telling her?

Test ❓

1. What is a 'vocation'?

2. What was God's message for Jesus when he was baptised by John?

3. How does Luke show that Jesus faced and made choices about his mission?

4. What two things are essential for discerning a Christian vocation?

5. Give two examples of how the Church supports and encourages the Christian vocation to proclaim the gospel.

Faith alive

Will you come and follow me,
if I but call your name?

This is the opening line of a song
from the Iona Community
(Wild Goose Music).
Find the song and listen to it,
or choose one that you know
to share with the class.

Key *words*

In your personal file
write down the
following words and
a one-sentence
explanation for each:

talent

quality

vocation

ministry

discern

Challenge
To see myself and others
as God sees.

Another step

What does Christian faith
contribute to a good sense
of self?

Pause for thought

*I cannot do what you do, and
you cannot do what I do, but
together we can do something
beautiful for God.*
(Mother Teresa)

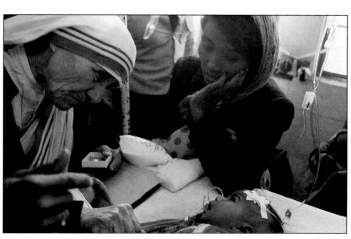

1C A sense of vocation

1D A lifetime's work

The Jones family

The Jones family were shattered when Baby Ieuan had an accident. It left him unable to walk. Yet today he is full of life and into mischief like any other toddler, and it's all thanks to his family. The doctors are amazed at his progress. His mum says it is thanks to Megan and Gwyn, his older sister and brother. They watched the way the physiotherapist exercised Ieuan's hands and feet. They learned how to help their mum to do this at home. This meant Ieuan had the extra attention he needed and made progress more quickly.

Why do you think his family helped Ieuan?
Do you think helping him helped each of them? In what ways?
What do you think it might have cost them? Remember, this means more than money.
How long do you think his family will care for Ieuan?

Think and talk in groups
Look at the pictures.

An 8,000m wheelchair race, Irvine, California.

A golden wedding celebration.

Seamus Heaney recieving a Nobel Award for Literature.

Work as a class

- Look through a selection of local and national newspapers to find examples of people using their gifts in the service of the community.
- Share and display your findings.
- If you could nominate someone for a lifelong service award, whom would you choose?
- Why would you choose the person?
- Write the speech that you would give at the presentation ceremony.

Pause for thought

What gifts are being used?

A call to live by the Spirit: the Sacrament of Confirmation

Confirmation is the second of the sacraments of initiation. It celebrates God the Holy Spirit and the gifts that help Christians to grow as members of the Church sharing its life and mission.

A group prepares for confirmation.

Check your learning
1. What is the first sacrament of initiation?
2. What does initiation mean?

In the celebration of Confirmation the laying on of hands and the anointing with the oil of chrism are the symbols of God's gift of the Holy Spirit. Jesus had promised his disciples that the Holy Spirit would come to them as guide and counsellor. He calls the Spirit the 'Paraclete' that is, 'the one who is called to one's side'.

The laying on of hands
The bishop and the priests who are celebrating with him extend their hands over all the candidates. The bishop prays that God will send the Holy Spirit to strengthen them.

The anointing with the oil of chrism
The bishop uses the oil of chrism to make the sign of the cross on the candidate's forehead and says:

Bishop: (Name) be sealed with the gift of the Holy Spirit.
Candidate: Amen.
Bishop: Peace be with you.
Candidate: And also with you.

Words we use
confirm – to make firm and definite, for example, to confirm a holiday booking or arrangement; to give your word to an agreement or bargain
signed and sealed – when an agreement is guaranteed by a person's signature and/or seal

Classwork

*Read the **Prayers of Confirmation** on Copymaster 6.*

A. *What hopes for the candidates are expressed in the prayers? Choose words or a sentence from the prayers that would be suitable for a Confirmation greeting card.*

B. *Using the prayers, present what the Church believes about God's gift and the role of the Holy Spirit in the life of a Christian. Use words, pictures or any other media. Your target audience is parents, and not all of them will be members of the Catholic Church. Remember, God's call includes freedom to respond. Christian life is a journey in which the Holy Spirit helps disciples to grow.*

C. *Write the bishop's homily. Think carefully about what you would want the candidates to remember, and don't make your homily too long. Use your ICT skills in presenting your work.*

Do you remember?

In the Eastern rite the three sacraments of initiation are celebrated together. In the Roman rite they are celebrated over several years. In the Eastern rite a person is confirmed as a baby. In the Roman rite Confirmation may be celebrated at any age. At present in England and Wales this happens at seven years old, 12, 13, 14 or 16 plus.

Immersion is used in the Eastern rite.

Group talk

Read the following statements and use them to discuss what the celebration of this sacrament would mean at each of the different ages for Confirmation.

Confirmation is a Sacrament:
- ◆ *that confers the power and the gifts of the Holy Spirit*
- ◆ *that completes Baptism*
- ◆ *of acceptance into the wider Christian community*
- ◆ *that strengthens communion with the Church*
- ◆ *that deepens relationship with Christ in the Eucharist*
- ◆ *that celebrates the Christian vocation and a personal response to God's call*
- ◆ *when the candidate formally makes his or her profession of faith.*

Water is poured over the baby's head in the Roman rite.

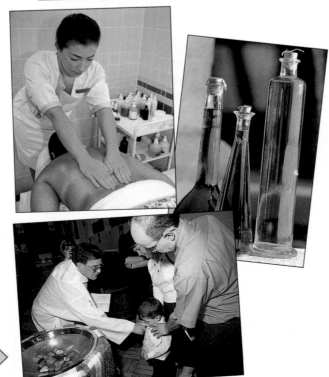

Oil as a symbol

Oil has many uses in the world.
Look at the pictures. What does the oil do in each case?
In the Old Testament, oil is also a symbol of God's blessing when someone is chosen for a special job.

1. In groups look up and read the following:
   1 Samuel 3; 1 Samuel 16:1–14.
2. For each story decide: whom did God choose? What special task was given to each person?

For the Church, anointing with the oil of chrism is a symbol of the new strength and beauty that God his Father gave Jesus when he raised him from the dead.

A name as a symbol

In the Scriptures a person is often given a new name as a sign of a calling or task. For example, Jacob's name was changed to Israel ('strong with God'). Jesus changed Simon's name to Peter, 'rock', because Peter was to be the leader among his disciples. Peter's successors as bishop of Rome became the Popes, leaders of the Catholic Church.

At baptism a person is welcomed by name when she or he becomes a member of the Church. Each person is baptised by name. This is their Christian name and that is why baptism is also known as 'christening'.

At Confirmation, candidates may use their baptismal name or choose a new name. This will be the name of a saint, who has lived according to the teachings of Christ and is an inspiration and example for them.

1. Make a short list of saints you could choose from for a confirmation name.
2. Give five reasons for your choice.
3. How would you have to change and grow to become like the one you chose?

Work as a class

Study and discuss these two verses of a modern Confirmation hymn. Here are some questions to help you:
1. What gifts of the Spirit does the hymn name?
2. How might you recognise these gifts in a person and in his or her life?
3. Brainstorm situations in which the Holy Spirit's gifts might help a Christian.
4. How are these gifts of the Holy Spirit revealed in the saints you named in your earlier work?

The gifts of the Spirit

The gift of the Holy Spirit
is the gift of God's great love.
To us comes the touch of healing
from the God of heav'n above;
joy and strength for our daily living,
trust and love for the work of giving
and the spirit of true forgiving each one.

Anointed, we are Christ's witness
in the walk of life each day,
a comfort and light to others
whom we meet along the way.
We will cherish your life within us,
show the mercy you show to sinners.
By your suffering, you chose to win us
from death.

'The Gift of the Holy Spirit', Sr Katherine Boschetti

Homework 🏛

Prepare a church notice inviting young people to apply to be confirmed. Think about the age group you are aiming at and the key message you want them to get.

1D A lifetime's work

Extension

Think back to the work you did on Baptism.

The oil of chrism is olive oil mixed with balsam, a sweet-smelling perfume. In the celebration of Baptism it symbolises the new relationship of the Christian with God. The priest says:

God the Father of our Lord Jesus Christ has freed you from sin, given you a new birth by water and the Holy Spirit, and welcomed you into his holy people. He now anoints you with the chrism of salvation. As Christ was anointed Priest, Prophet and King, so may you live always as a member of his body, sharing everlasting life.

In Confirmation, the anointing with chrism symbolises the coming of the Holy Spirit. Each baptised person is called to live in the Spirit of Jesus. The gifts of the Spirit help the person to live in communion with Jesus and his body, the Church.

♦ Think about ways in which every baptised person can be more like Christ, the priest, prophet and king. Here are some ideas to help you:

as a priest look for and celebrate what is holy in life; proclaiming the good news, for example, being faithful in prayer, giving oneself in the service of others

as a prophet open to God; speaking God's word to people and speaking of people to God; for example, speaking the truth, standing up for belief, explaining what you believe, giving good example

as a king taking responsibility for the good of the community; serving others as Jesus did; for example, helping at home, caring for the poor and sick; spending time with others.

♦ With a partner, think of some ways in which a baptised person could use the gifts of the Spirit and share the mission of Jesus in these ways if he or she were:
(a) a 10-year-old   (b) a teenager
(c) a mother or father.

♦ Share your ideas with the class.

♦ Together draw up a three point action plan for each person.

Words we use

salvation – God's saving work in Jesus freeing people *from* death *for* life

priest – ordained to the service of God's people; in the Old Testament offers sacrifice in the Temple

prophet – someone guided by the Holy Spirit; speaking God's word to people

king – in the Scriptures the king is the shepherd of God's people

Links

Notice on the parish notice-board:

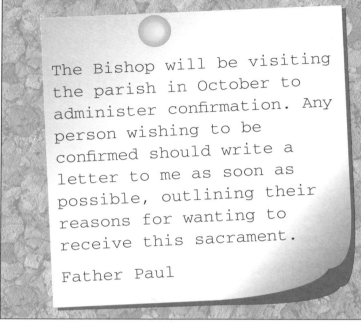

The Bishop will be visiting the parish in October to administer confirmation. Any person wishing to be confirmed should write a letter to me as soon as possible, outlining their reasons for wanting to receive this sacrament.

Father Paul

Write the letter to the priest.

Test ❓

1. *Give two examples of gifts shared for the good of others.*
2. *What does the oil of chrism symbolise?*
3. *List the gifts of the Holy Spirit.*
4. *What does the bishop pray at the laying on of hands? What does his action symbolise?*
5. *What promises are made at Confirmation?*

Challenge
Confirmation is Pentecost in the life of each Christian. What difference does the gift of the Holy Spirit make?

Faith alive

Come, O Creator Spirit,
Visit our minds,
Fill with your grace
The hearts you have created.

(From the Hymn at Evening Prayer for Pentecost Sunday)

Key words

In your personal file write down the following words and a one-sentence explanation for each:

Confirmation

anointing

chrism

candidate

Another step
How do the promises at Confirmation build on the baptismal promises?

Pause for thought

"You are the place where God speaks."

What do you think this means? How can God speak through you?

1D A lifetime's work

1E Back to the future

Many happy returns

On your Birthday
Fly **high**
Live **large**
Dream **big**
It's a brand new year and it's all yours.

This is your day

Have a perfect birthday!

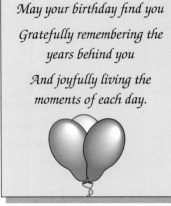

May your birthday find you
Gratefully remembering the years behind you
And joyfully living the moments of each day.

A day of joy and happiness
A day of fun and friends
And in the days of the year ahead
Good times, good health, good friends.

Look at the birthday card wishes.

1. What do these good wishes tell you about what a birthday celebrates?
2. How are the past, present and future part of a birthday? Some of these words might help you: remember, remembering, celebrate, celebrating, looking forward, wishing, hoping.
3. Compose a verse for a birthday card for someone in your family, or perhaps a friend. Try to get across the idea that birthdays are about remembering, celebrating and hopes for the future.

Is your birthday anything like this? ***Birthday scene:*** *Copymaster* [7]

Check your learning ✓✓

Which of the following phrases best describe the Church's message at Advent and why?

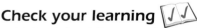

Alleluia! Christ is risen! *Come to Bethlehem and see him!* *Christ the Lord is risen today!*

Joy to the world, the Lord has come! *Prepare the way of the Lord!*

Advent

Advent is the first season of the Church's Year. 'Advent' means 'coming'. For four weeks Christians are called to examine their lives and prepare to celebrate the coming of Jesus. The prayers, readings and customs of the season help them to think about:

the past – what happened before Jesus' birth when people looked forward to his coming

the present – how the Church is getting ready for this year's celebration

the future – looking forward to the time when Jesus will come again.

John the Baptist

One of the Church's Advent figures is John the Baptist. Luke's Gospel says that John learned about how special Jesus was going to be whilst he and Jesus were each still in their mothers' wombs. (Check Luke 1:39–45.)

People called John the Baptist a prophet. The prophets of the Old Testament spoke God's word to the people. They called them to remember the past, examine the present and prepare for the future. They spoke in words and in symbolic actions. They proclaimed God's message for the people and called them back to trust in God's promises and faithfulness to God's law. Prophets look to the future with hope, trusting in God. This enables them to speak with insight, but does not mean they can 'see' the future. Even prophets have questions and find God's ways surprising.

Bible Alive: *the baptism of Jesus.*

As a class, build a profile of John the Baptist.
Work in groups using the Church's gospel readings.

	Cycle A	Cycle B	Cycle C
Second Sunday of Advent	Matthew 3:1–12	Mark 1:1–8	Luke 3:1–6
Third Sunday of Advent	Matthew 11:2–11	John 1:6–8, 19–28	Luke 3:10–18
Second Sunday after Christmas	John 1:1–18	John 1:1–18	John 1:1–18
The Baptism of the Lord	Matthew 3:13–17	Mark 1:7–11	Luke 3:15–16, 21–22 (Also Luke 7:18–21)

In each group

1. Use your readings to collect evidence of:
   John's way of life; his trust in God; his hope in God's promises; his uncertainty and questions; his faith in Jesus.

2. Decide what message these readings give about: John the Baptist; Jesus; God the Father; God the Holy Spirit.

3. Decide how you will present your profile. You may use some or all of the following: words, symbols, music, mime, drama, dance, artwork.

4. Present your profiles for the class.

Be ready!

John the Baptist prepared people for the coming of Jesus. People asked him for advice. He warned them about what had gone wrong in the past. He encouraged them to change so that they would be ready for the future.

Read Luke 3:1–20.

1. What was John's message?
2. How do you think people felt when they heard this?
3. What kind of people came to John?
4. What advice did he give them?
5. How did this challenge them?
6. What did John say about himself?

Pause for thought

*Find and listen to the song from **Godspell**, 'Prepare ye the way of the Lord' and/or watch it on video.*

≡ Homework 🏛 ≡

What is there in John's preaching that makes him a good Advent figure for the Church? Give as many reasons as you can and back up your ideas using examples of people today who might go to John for advice.

Lighting the Advent wreath.

Someone is coming

When Luke uses the story of John to introduce Jesus, he is making it clear from the start that Jesus' coming is part of God's plan for all people. The Church reads the prophecies of the Old Testament as messages about the coming of Jesus.

Use your Bible skills to look up the following references: Jeremiah 33:14–16; Isaiah 7:14, 9:2–7, 11:1–3; Micah 5:2.

Now look up these references from Matthew's gospel: 1:18–23, 2:1–6, 2:16–18 and 3:1–6.

Think and talk

Matthew was probably writing for Jewish Christians. How does this explain the importance of the prophecies in his story of the infancy of Jesus?

≡ Classwork ✍ ≡

A. *'Who is this Jesus?' Design an Advent poster for the outside of a church to encourage people to come in.*

B. *Using what you have read, collect evidence under two headings: 'Historical facts' and 'Promises'. Write an Advent slogan for a banner to hang on the lectern where the readers proclaim the Word of God.*

C. *List the ways Matthew uses the prophets' messages to help his readers understand more about Jesus.*

Be alert!

The imagery in the prophecies of Isaiah and Jeremiah you have studied shows how the writers try to find language to express the wonder of God and the great things God will do. There is also a sense of the unexpected. God can be a God of surprises. Zachariah, a priest in the Temple, was probably surprised when his son John began preaching in the desert. Mary's vocation certainly surprised her. In the Matthew passages you explored you will have seen more surprises. Joseph was called to trust God and accept Mary's child as the saviour of his people. The wise men from the East came to worship a great king and found a baby.

Advent is a waiting time, a season of expectation. The Church calls Christians to remember the unexpected ways of God and to be open to the mystery of God revealed in Jesus.

Study the words of this modern hymn.
How does the imagery it uses call to mind the 'unexpected' God?

1. *God beyond our dreams,*
   you have stirred in us a mem'ry;
   you have placed your pow'rful spirit
   in the hearts of human kind.

   Refrain:
   All around us we have known you,
   all creation lives to hold you,
   in our living and our dying
   we are bringing you to birth.

2. *God, beyond all names,*
   you have made us in your image;
   we are like you, we reflect you;
   we are woman, we are man.

3. *God, beyond all words,*
   all creation tells your story;
   you have shaken with our laughter,
   you have trembled with our tears.

4. *God, beyond all time,*
   you are labouring within us.
   We are moving, we are changing
   in your spirit, ever new.

5. *God of tender care,*
   you have cradled us in goodness,
   you have mothered us in wholeness,
   you have loved us into birth.

   'God Beyond All Names', Bernadette Farrell

Worship at Christmas.

Think and talk

What 'picture' of God do you get from this hymn?
What do you find new, challenging, encouraging, puzzling, unhelpful, surprising?
What links can you make to the work you have done in this unit?
For example, Jesus, God made man, living a human life; the unique vocation of each person, the Holy Spirit who gifts each person.

Links

Pause for thought

Lighting the candles on the Advent wreath is a way of looking forward to Christmas.

Use the work you have done in this section to write a prayer for each of the four Sundays of Advent. How will your prayers build up to the lighting of the Jesus candle at the centre?

Challenge
'Let God be God.' What do you think this means?
Why do you think people find this difficult?

Test ?

1. *What is Advent?*

2. *What is a prophet?*

3. *Name two prophets whose promises are applied to Jesus.*

4. *How did John the Baptist prepare people for Jesus' coming?*

5. *Explain how past, present and future are part of the Church's Advent season.*

Key words

In your personal file write down the following words and a one-sentence explanation for each:

Advent

hope

future

prophet

Faith alive

How do the words and music of these two songs capture the mood of Advent?

Wait for the Lord: his day is near.
Wait for the Lord: be strong, take heart.
(Taizé chant)

1. *Praise to you, O Christ, our Saviour,*
   Word of the Father, calling us to life;
   Son of God who leads us to freedom:
   Glory to you, Lord Jesus Christ!

2. *You are the Word who calls us out of darkness;*
   You are the Word who leads us into light;
   You are the Word who brings us through the desert:
   Glory to you, Lord Jesus Christ!

3. *You are the one whom prophets hoped and longed for;*
   You are the one who speaks to us today;
   You are the one who leads us to our future:
   Glory to you, Lord Jesus Christ!

4. *You are the Word who binds us and unites us;*
   You are the Word who calls us to be one;
   You are the Word who teaches us forgiveness:
   Glory to you, Lord Jesus Christ!

'Your Words are Spirit and Life', Bernadette Farrell

The People of God

What's in a name?

In the modern world, all big companies rely upon 'brand recognition' – getting their name recognised.

1. Which do you think is the most famous brand name in the world?
2. Who do you think is best at promoting their name?
3. Why is name recognition so important?
4. Names and logos go together. Think of a group or organisation that does not even need a name because its logo is universally recognised.

> **In this section of our work we will be learning:**
>
> ◆ about the power of a name
> ◆ about the Exodus and why the Church is named 'The People of God'.

The people of ...

Often a news item will begin 'The people of …' Or someone being interviewed will say "People are worried/relieved/surprised".

1. Brainstorm 'people'.
2. How many different meanings/ways of using the word did you find?
3. What is it that forms and unites a people?
4. What helps a nation to begin to think of itself as a people?
5. What harms the unity of such a group?

Check your learning ✓✓

Try to match these names for the Church with the correct image.

In each case, does the image help you to understand the meaning of the name?

Now explain in your own words what you think each of the five names mean.

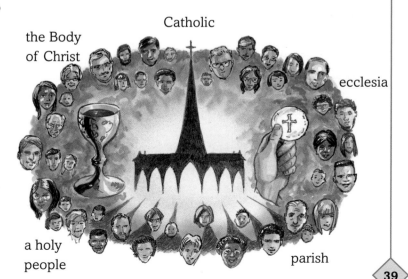

the Body of Christ

Catholic

ecclesia

a holy people

parish

The People of God

 2

A key name given to the Church is 'The People of God'. These are the people all over the world that God gathers to be one community. Let's examine where the name comes from. (Remember: Christian tradition uses BC – Before Christ – and AD – the year of the Lord. Jewish tradition uses BCE – before the common era – and CE – common era.)

A long story

1. Genesis: Beginnings circa 2000 BC

God calls Abraham to lead his Hebrew family from Ur to the land of Canaan. He is the first with whom God makes a covenant.
Abraham's son Isaac is a sign of God's blessing.
The call of Abraham: Genesis 12:1–9.
The covenant: Genesis 15; 17:1–21.
A test of faithfulness: Genesis 22.

2. Eighteenth to fifteenth centuries BC

Isaac's son Jacob is a fighter all his life. He earns the name 'Israel', meaning 'you have struggled with God': Genesis 32:22–30.
He has 12 sons.
Joseph, Jacob's favourite son, is sold into slavery by his jealous brothers.
In Egypt he rises from being a slave to become the trusted servant of Pharaoh, the ruler of Egypt.
Joseph's story: Genesis 37:2–36; 39–47.

8. 63 BC
The Roman general Pompey captures Jerusalem.

9. 37 BC–AD 4
Herod the Great appointed king by the Romans.

7. Sixth to first centuries BC
The exiles return. The Temple is rebuilt: Nehemiah 8:1–11.
There is still no peace. Neighbouring powers fight over the kingdom: a time of persecution and fighting.

10. 6–4 BC
Jesus born in Bethlehem.

3. Thirteenth century BC

From welcome and honoured guests the Israelites become an ethnic minority, oppressed slaves in Egypt. God chooses Moses to lead them out of slavery.

The Exodus is the escape from Egypt. The covenant is renewed at Sinai. Moses leads the people to the land that God had promised Abraham.

4. Twelfth to eleventh centuries BC

Judges and prophets lead God's people: Joshua, Samson, Samuel, Elijah.

The people plead for a king and Samuel anoints Saul as God's chosen king: 1 Samuel 10:1.

5. circa 1010–931BC

David is Israel's greatest king. He is remembered as a writer of psalms, a warrior, a king who loved God and his people and a man able to admit his sin and ask forgiveness: 1 Samuel 16:1–13.

Solomon is David's son. He builds a marvellous Temple in Jerusalem. He is famous for his wisdom: 1 Kings 3:5–14.

6. Ninth to fifth centuries BC

The kingdom is divided: Israel in the north and Judah in the south. First, Assyrian armies come from the east. Then come the Babylonians.

In around 598 the Babylonian King, Nebuchadnezzar, deports the people of Judah.

Read Psalm 137, The Ballad of the Exiles.

In 587BC Jerusalem is captured and the Temple looted.

Group task

Use the timeline to identify key people and events in the history of the People of God. Each group choose one person from the timeline. Prepare five points explaining why he or she is a key figure in the story of God's People.

2A The People of God

Escape to freedom

2

In the Scriptures, the story of the Exodus is the great sign of God's faithfulness. God rescues his People. God is faithful to the covenant with Abraham. The covenant is a blessing.

Group task one: The Exodus

1. Research the story of the escape from Egypt. Here are references to help you.

God calls Moses	Exodus 3:1–8
God tells Moses his name	Exodus 3:11–15
God is faithful	Exodus 6:3–7
The Plagues	Exodus 7:11
The Passover	Exodus 12
The Exodus	Exodus 12
Across the Red Sea	Exodus 14:21–31
The Covenant renewed	Exodus 20:19–20

*Passage through the Red Sea,
Julius Schnorr von Carolsfeld, c 1860.*

2. Make a list of the symbols and symbolic actions; for example, the unleavened bread, the blood on the door posts.

3. Decide on a way to present your findings. Choose one of the following suggestions or another way of your own choice. Use your ICT and English skills.

- Each group chooses one part of the story and dramatises it. Record your presentation on tape or video. Present it at a year assembly.
- Write a series of diary entries to tell the story in the words of different people who were part of the story; for example, Moses, Pharaoh, an Egyptian soldier, an Israelite mother, an Egyptian or Israelite boy or girl.
- Put together a newspaper special feature: 'Escape to freedom'.

The light of Christ makes holy the waters of baptism.

Work as a class

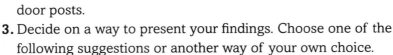

4. Discuss what you have learned about
   (a) God   (b) what it means to be the People of God.
5. Make two lists to show the privileges and responsibilities of the covenant.

Another step

What does the symbolic language add to the story?

Group task two: A new Covenant

The Exodus is a significant event for both Jews and Christians.
The Church celebrates Jesus' death and resurrection as his Passover from
death to new life. The gospels record Jesus' last Passover meal and his
words: "This is the new covenant." (Luke 22:14–20)

At the Easter Vigil, in the Liturgy of Readings the Church recalls the
history of the People of God. The readings and psalms celebrate the first
Covenant and give thanks for God's faithfulness. They recall the
faithfulness and unfaithfulness of the Israelites and their transformation
into the People of God. For the Church, Jesus is 'the new Moses', leading
God's people from the slavery of sin and death to the freedom of new life.

Classwork

Retelling the story

A. Work in groups, with one or two readings each.
What do the reading and psalm say about:
God and the covenant   faithfulness and unfaithfulness
how the people are changed and transformed
the privileges and responsibilities of being the People of God.

First reading	Genesis 1:1–2:2	Psalm 103:1-2, 5–6, 10, 12–14, 24, 35
Second reading	Genesis 22:1–18	Psalm 15:5, 8–11.
Third reading	Exodus 14:15–15:1	Song of Moses Exodus 15:1–6, 17–18
Fourth reading	Isaiah 54:5–14	Psalm 29:4–6,11–13.
Fifth reading	Isaiah 55:1–11	Song of Salvation Isaiah 12:2–6
Sixth reading	Baruch 3:9–15, 32–4:4	Psalm 18:8–11
Seventh reading	Ezekiel 36:16–28	Psalms 41:3, 5; 42:3–4

Liturgy of the Word Romans 6:3–11 Psalm 117:1–2, 16–17, 22–23

Gospel: (A) Matthew 28:1–10; (B) Mark 16:1–7; (C) Luke 24:1–12.

Present your findings to the class.

B. Design a timeline of events from the First Reading to the Gospel.
Your target audience are Y6 students. You want them to understand
the key people and events in the story of the People of God.

C. Why do you think the Church retells this story in the Easter
Liturgy? Give two reasons why it is significant for the People of
the New Covenant.

Homework 🏠

People of God:
Copymaster [8]

Pause for thought

*God is more anxious to bless
than we are to be blessed.*

Links

Pause for thought

The People of God are chosen people.
The People of God pass through the waters to freedom.
The People of God are a covenant people.
The People of God live by the Law of love and freedom.
The People of God are a sign of God the faithful One.

> *Challenge*
> The first step, 'freedom *from*', has to be followed by the second, 'freedom *to*'.

Faith alive

> *Amazing grace! How sweet the sound*
> *that saved a wretch like me.*
> *I once was lost, but now am found;*
> *was blind, but now I see.*
> *'Twas grace that taught my heart to fear,*
> *and grace my fears relieved.*
> *How precious did that grace*
> *appear, the hour I first believed.*
> *Through many dangers, toils and snares*
> *I have already come.*
> *'Tis grace hath brought me safe thus far,*
> *and grace will lead me home.*
> *The Lord has promised good to me;*
> *his word my hope secures.*
> *He will my shield and portion be*
> *as long as life endures.*

The author of this hymn was John Newton (1725–1807).
He was a sea captain and became involved in the slave trade.
Do you think there are echoes of these experiences in his hymn?

Test ❓

1. *Who were the first People of God?*
2. *Why is Sinai important in the story of the People of God?*
3. *Give two reasons why the Church calls itself the 'People of God'.*
4. *What is the 'new covenant'?*
5. *Name two responsibilities and two privileges of being the People of God.*

Key *words*

In your personal file write down the following words and a one-sentence explanation for each:

covenant

Exodus

Passover

freedom

faithful

Pause for thought

'Grace' – the power of God in human lives.

Another step

Write five points for each side in a debate on the subject 'To call the Church the People of God leaves out more than half the world'.

In search of wholeness

When it all goes wrong

Form 8B had settled well into the life of their new school. They got on well with one another and everyone had at least one friend. Whenever anyone in the class was upset or worried, there would always be someone on hand offering support or help. They worked well together and never left anyone out of class activities such as fund-raising. They made new class members feel welcome and volunteered for any jobs that needed doing. It was great to belong to the class. Until … things started to go missing in the class. First it was pencil cases, then PE kit, then money. Gradually everyone started to suspect everyone else and no one would leave anything around. The class was no longer happy. The team spirit had gone.

What's behind the headlines?

Divorce Rate Soars

Peace Talks Break Down

Children Taken into Care

Third World Debt: Not Our Problem

She Betrayed Her Country

In this section of our work we will be learning:

◆ about the struggle involved in living in relationship with others
◆ about the Church's two sacraments of healing.

Think and talk in groups

1. What was life like in 8B before things went wrong?
2. How had they achieved this?
3. What changed and why?
4. What happened next?
5. How did they feel?
6. How should they go about restoring relationships and unity?

Refugees in their own land.

Choose one headline and write a one-column news item for a newspaper or record a two-minute news slot for a TV news bulletin.

You will need to include:
◆ what relationships have broken down
◆ what promises have been broken
◆ what injustice has been done
◆ what the consequences are for all the people involved.

Use as resources for your work at least two of the following: national newspaper, international newspaper, TV or radio current affairs programmes. As a class: discuss your ideas.

"Yes" to new life

In 2A you studied the Easter Vigil and the New Covenant. Easter is the high point of the Church's year, the Church's greatest feast. In recent times the tradition of adult baptisms at the Easter Vigil has been revived and gives a powerful sign of the meaning of Easter. The death and resurrection of Jesus means freedom *from* sin and *for* new life. The Scripture readings lead from the waters of creation to a new creation in the waters of baptism. The newly-baptised are welcomed as children of God into the community of disciples, the family of the Church.

Check your learning

Why are Christians called 'the Easter People'?
Give two examples of living as Easter People.

At Easter, the renewal of baptismal promises unites the Church in a renewal of faith and commitment to say "no" to sin and "yes" to new life. This is a lifelong challenge. The Church supports Christians in the struggle to be faithful in several ways. Each year the season of Lent is a time of renewal, repentance and preparation for the joy of Easter. Throughout the year the sacraments of healing renew and strengthen communion.

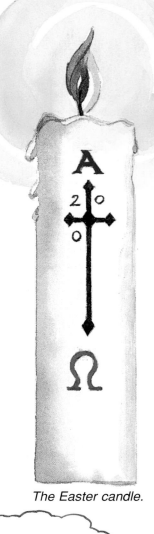

The Easter candle.

Lent: A spotlight on faithfulness

The spiritual struggle often means choosing between right and wrong.
Everyone struggles in this way at times. St Paul, writing to the Romans, told them about his struggle. (Romans 7:18, 19, 23)

On Ash Wednesday, Lent begins with the blessing with ashes. Each person hears the call to 'Turn away from sin and be faithful to the gospel'. This can mean 'giving up' or 'taking on', choosing to do something positive as a way of developing self-control.

I don't do the good I want to do; instead, I do the evil that I don't want to do.

Turn away from sin! Turn away from what?

1. In a group, look at this list. Remember that sin is a deliberate, personal choice to break God's commandment: 'Love God, and love your neighbour as yourself'.

2. Decide which of the following a Christian might decide to turn away from in Lent.

spreading rumours

repeating gossip

telling lies

supporting CAFOD

swearing

using God's name without respect

going to the disco

staying up late

not going to church on Sunday

breaking a promise

giving up chocolate

refusing to share your sweets

bullying

spraying graffiti

3. Make a list of what a Christian might choose as a form of Lenten prayer, fasting or almsgiving that would express love of God, of neighbour and of yourself.

4. Share your lists with another group.

5. Make a class list.

6. Choose two or three examples from the list and explain what changes a Christian would need to make in order to live 'faithful to the gospel'.

2B In search of wholeness

Sacraments of healing

The sacraments of healing are Reconciliation and the Anointing of the Sick. They recognise the struggle involved in living the new life of communion with God and with others. They restore or renew communion.

Sin is a separation. Remember the parable of the prodigal son (Year 7). It was his utter isolation in the pigsty and his longing for his father's house that brought him back. Sickness, also, can bring separation and loneliness. The sacraments of healing bring wholeness, God's gifts of comfort, strength and reassurance that the gift of life in Baptism is forever.

A priest and a penitent.

The Sacrament of Reconciliation brings God's gift of forgiveness. It enables Christians to be honest about naming and facing their struggles and their sins. It is a time to recognise the damage sin does to relationship with God and with others. It is a time to turn back to God in sorrow and trust and to receive God's gift of forgiveness.

A penitential service.

The Sacrament of Reconciliation

Step One: Welcome and invitation to trust in God's love.

Step Two: Listening to or calling to mind the Word of God.

Step Three: Confession (naming and acknowledging sins to a priest).
             Prayer of Sorrow (asking for forgiveness).
             Absolution (the priest speaks the words of forgiveness).

Step Four: Thanksgiving for God's love and forgiveness.

As a sign of true sorrow and conversion, 'a change of heart', the person accepts a penance. This will involve making amends in some way, by prayer, self-denial or service of others.

Prayers for the Sacrament of Reconciliation:

Copymaster ⑨ Study the words of the prayers from the Sacrament.

What do they tell us about God's faithfulness and Christian faithfulness?

≡ Homework 🏛 ≡

Recognising evil: *Copymaster* ⑩

Pause for thought 💭

The Greek word for conversion is metanoia.

It means 'a change of mind'. In a Christian sense it means the kind of change of heart that turns a person away from sin and to God.

Turn to me, O turn and
be saved,
For I am God, there is no other;
  none beside me.
I call your name.

What do these words say about the Sacrament of Reconciliation?

The Sacrament of the Anointing of the Sick

Illness can be a time when people struggle to make sense of life and feel alone and helpless. They can feel cut off from their family and friends and, sometimes, it can seem as if God also has abandoned them.

Why did this happen to me?

If God is loving, why do children die?

I do love her, but I just can't cope with her being ill.

Discuss what the struggle would be in each of these situations. How might they add to a sense of isolation?

The mission of Jesus is to bring wholeness. He calls people back to a right relationship with God and with one another. In Palestine, 2,000 years ago, he healed the sick and his miracles were signs of the wholeness that God wants for all people and of God's presence with them. Today, in the sacraments, believers meet the same Jesus, and the Church, in his name, continues his healing mission.

Read:
Luke 4:38–41
Matthew 4:23–25
Mark 1:40–44.

Jesus Opens the Eyes of a Man Born Blind, Duccio, 1278–1319.

Prepare a feature for a popular magazine using these stories and others you may know about Jesus the Healer from Galilee.
Decide what angle you will take about Jesus and his message.

The Church continues this healing work of Jesus through the Sacrament of the Anointing of the Sick. In this sacrament the laying on of hands and anointing with oil are symbols of the gift of God's love, comfort and strength that this sacrament brings. The celebration of the sacrament within Mass is a sign of the love and support of the community.

Pope John Paul II anointing the sick at Southwark Cathedral.

Prayers for the Sacrament of Anointing of the Sick within Mass: *Copymaster* [11]
Using the prayers, write a paragraph to explain how they would bring comfort and strength to
(a) the sick person and
(b) the person's family or friends.

Class project: HCPT – The Pilgrimage Trust

Not everyone who goes to Lourdes is cured of their illness, but the vast majority of people, sick and disabled people and helpers, talk of the unity and joy of being together and the strength that comes from the support and example of others.

Contact the HCPT main or local office. If possible, invite an HCPT helper to talk about his or her experience of travelling to Lourdes with children with special needs. Here are some ideas of what to include in your project: factual details: address; explanation of what HCPT is and what it does; views and opinions from people involved as helpers, passengers and their families.

Classwork

A. Copy the following paragraph into your book. Complete each of the sentences using the words listed below.
The gifts of the Sacraments of … and the Anointing of the … are God's … and mercy in times of struggle.
… is a time to recognise the damage … does to relationship with … and …
The laying on of … and anointing with … are … of God's love, … and … .
hands   Reconciliation   others   oil   God   love
strength   Sick   comfort   sin   Confession   signs

B. Plan a Service for the Anointing of the Sick for a parish. Choose hymns and readings. What 'good news' does the Church want sick people to hear? How will you advertise your service? Should housebound people be invited? Will some people need transport to get to the church?

C. Read: Luke 9:1–2; Acts 28:7–10; James 5:13–15. What evidence do you find in these stories to justify the Church's belief that the healing power of Jesus has been handed on?

Test ❓

1. What are the Church's two sacraments of healing?
2. Why are there two sacraments of healing?
3. Give an example of a sin a Christian might turn away from in Lent.
4. What are the steps of the Sacrament of Reconciliation?
5. What two symbols are used in the Anointing of the Sick?

Pause for thought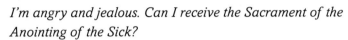

I'm angry and jealous. Can I receive the Sacrament of the Anointing of the Sick?

Challenge
I'm not hurting anyone. This affects me and no one else. How can it be a sin?

Key *words*

In your personal file write down the following words and a one-sentence explanation for each:

sin

forgiveness

reconciliation

repentance

metanoia

mercy

Anointing of the Sick

Another step
Plan a commentary to go with a video of these moments in the celebration of the Anointing of the Sick. Write or record your commentary.

Faith alive

The Lord is my light and my help; whom shall I fear?

The Lord is the stronghold of my life; before whom shall I shrink?

Psalm 27:1

Actions speak louder than words.

2B In search of wholeness

2C Saviour of the world

It's the way we speak

> Saved by the bell!

> You saved my life!

> Saved from making a fool of myself!

> What a save!

People use these expressions every day. Give examples of when each of these sayings might be used.

In this section of our work we will be learning:

◆ about some ways people need to 'be saved'
◆ that Luke's gospel proclaims Jesus is the Saviour of the world
◆ about the challenge to be one world.

It's the way things happen

We Won Through!

Sea Rescue! It's a miracle he's alive

They're Home!

She's Safe!

Behind these headlines are stories of people who got themselves into situations where they needed help.

Choose one and write or tell the story. Remember that sometimes people have to go through difficulties to reach safety.

Pause for thought

The flood waters were rising fast. The passengers in a boat saw a man clinging to a roof. "Room for one more," they shouted. "Come on!"
'No thanks,' shouted the man, "I trust in God to save me."
The waters rose higher and a lifeboat came along. The lifeboat men called to the man to come down. He refused their help with the same answer. By now the water was lapping round his feet, but he said the same to a helicopter and its crew.
They flew away. The waters rose and the man drowned.
When he got to heaven he complained to God. "I trusted in you and you didn't help me."
"Well," said God, "I did send two boats and a helicopter."
Don't be too quick to decide how God will act.

Check your learning

True or false:

1. 'Jesus' is a Hebrew name. It means 'God saves' or 'Saviour'.
2. Being saved means going to heaven.
3. Only people who go to church on Sunday will go to heaven.

The Christian way

For Christians, 'being saved' or 'salvation' has a particular meaning. It means God's gift of love and life and what God does to bring these gifts to fulfilment. The Church believes that Jesus' life, death and resurrection are actions that save the world *from* sin and death and *for* life that is *eternal*. Remember your work in 2A (p. 42). The covenant was God's commitment to his People and the People's commitment to the commandments, a new way of life. Luke's gospel emphasises Jesus as the Saviour of all the world, not just the Jewish People of God. This is what you will study next.

eternal: everlasting, sharing God's life now and for ever

Who was Luke?
Tradition tells us:

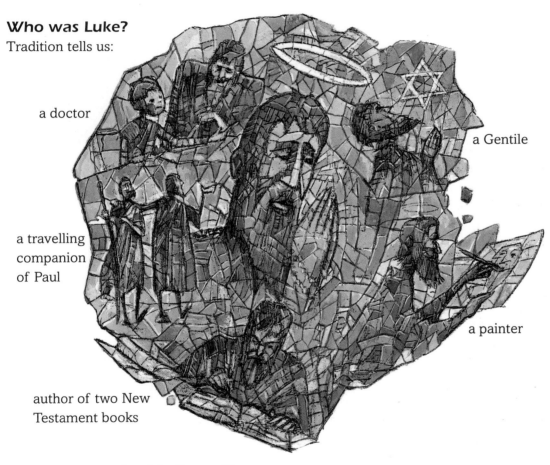

a doctor

a Gentile

a travelling
companion
of Paul

a painter

author of two New
Testament books

Why did he write his Gospel?
◆ to show that the Good News is for all people, not just the Jews
◆ to show Jesus' care for the poor and outcasts
◆ to show that Jesus came for the salvation of all people.

> *Info box*
> Luke addresses both his books to Theophilus. This Greek name means 'lover of God'.

Saviour for all people

2

Look up each of the following occasions when
Jesus met different people.
Who is being saved: 'from what' and 'for what'?
What does Jesus say and do?
How would their lives have changed?

The widow at Nain 7: 11–15

*The woman with a
   haemorrhage 8: 43–48*

The call of Levi 5: 27–32

The boy with epilepsy 9: 38–43

The sinful woman 7: 36–50

Saved for ever

There is one story in Luke's gospel that helps us to understand the kind of
saving Jesus brings. Read Luke 23:39–43.

Think and talk

Note: *paradise* = heaven. Remember Genesis: the garden of Eden.
1. How were the two men crucified with Jesus different in their behaviour?
2. What did each ask Jesus to do?
3. How did Jesus respond?
4. What is Luke's message about Jesus?
Agree one sentence that sums up the message of this event.

Classwork

A. *From the work you have done, produce a five-minute report on any one of
these events for a weekend current affairs radio programme.
Interview the person saved by Jesus. Include some of the reactions of others
to what Jesus was doing.*

B. *You are thinking about becoming a disciple of Jesus. You have just
witnessed Jesus' saving power in the above events. What questions do you
have for Jesus about being the Saviour? What concerns do you have?*

C. *You are preparing a booklet about Jesus the Saviour for a Jerusalem youth
magazine. Plan a cover photograph. Who would be in it? List the types of
people. Write brief pen portraits of each, including what Jesus offers them.
Tip: Remember Luke's message.*

One world

Luke's second book tells how the message of salvation was taken to all peoples.
Read Acts 26:23, 28:28

Think and talk in groups

Imagine that Luke is writing his gospel today. Which groups would he include and how would he show Jesus treating them?
Which groups of people need saving today? Who are the marginalised in our society?

Present your ideas under the heading: *The message of salvation: then and now.* Use words, pictures, spider graphs, drama, posters.

Jesus was involved with ordinary people and the Good News he came to bring was for everyone. Luke tells the story with a bias towards the poor and the marginalised of society. Jesus tried to break down the barriers that separated people and overcome prejudice. The Church continues this work today in partnership with many organisations. These exist to improve the way of life of the under-privileged and work towards 'One World'.

One World Week enables people to learn about global issues and to take action for global justice.

One World Week

Every year during the month of October, from Cardiff to Kenya, Zambia to Oswestry, Lahore to Liverpool, Christians everywhere are invited to celebrate One World Week (OWW).

These are some titles of the campaigns of the week during the last twenty-two years:

– Breaking Barriers
– Women and Children First
– Recipes for Justice
– Listen for a Change
– Value for People
– Trading Places, Linking Lives.

The week:
◆ brings together local people to act on global issues
◆ builds a movement of globally aware and active citizens
◆ makes an impact on decision makers locally, nationally and internationally.

Class Project: One World Week

1. Look at the campaign titles.
   Who do you think the campaigns aimed to help? What needs do you think they were trying to meet?
2. Find out about One World Week. Prepare a letter to the Campaign Office. What information do you want? What questions will you need to ask to get it?
3. Plan your own One World Week in school. Choose a theme and a message you want to get across. Is there a visitor or speaker you could invite?
4. Design a poster for your One World Week.

☰ Homework 🏛 ☰

Prepare for your headteacher three reasons why your year group should support the work of One World Week.

2C Saviour of the world

Links

Pause for thought

All the ends of the earth have seen the power of God.
(Psalm 98 verse 3)

Choose a song in praise of Jesus the Saviour that your school uses for prayer and worship. Write down the key word or phrase that makes you choose this song.

Test ?

1. Explain 'saved *from*' and 'saved *for*'.
2. Why did Luke write his gospel?
3. Give two examples from Luke's gospel that show how Jesus saves people.
4. In what ways are miracles 'signs' of Jesus the Saviour?
5. How does the saving work of Jesus continue in the world today?

Key *words*

In your personal file write down the following words and a one-sentence explanation for each:

One World

marginalised

prejudice

salvation

Challenge
To be saved is to live a new life.

Faith alive

1. Jesus, Lamb of God, and source of life,
   Jesus, loving bearer of our sins:
   Hear our prayer, have mercy;
   Hear our prayer, have mercy;
   Give us your peace.

2. Jesus, Son of God and Son of Man,
   Jesus, true redeemer of the world:

3. Jesus Christ, our Way, our Truth, our Life,
   Jesus Christ, our living Cornerstone:

4. Jesus, Lord of life and Lord of light,
   Jesus, here in form of bread and wine:

(For Lent)
Jesus, source of everlasting life,
Jesus, source of reconciling love:

Jesus, by whose suffering we are healed,
Jesus man of sorrows, friend of grief:

Jesus, crucified, transcending time,
Jesus, Saviour, by whose death we live:

'Jesus, Lamb of God', Paul Inwood

You might like to find this litany for the breaking of the bread and look up the Easter verses.

Another step

Choose two of the following people or groups and identify at least two verses from the hymn that they might pray: the widow of Naim, Levi, the repentant criminal, Christian volunteers in the Third World. Explain the reasons for your choices.

An ancient symbol of Christ the Savior.

People of spirit and truth

Where will it end?

The words in Box 2 are often the result of the attitudes in Box 1.

Match the words. You may find you use some more than once.

In this section of our work we will be learning:

◆ about the importance of a sense of personal worth
◆ about the Church's teaching about sin in human life
◆ about conscience.

Box 1
intolerance
spitefulness
tolerance
scorn
bullying
prejudice
racism
lies

Box 2
oppression
unhappiness
discrimination
persecution
injustice
hatred
suffering
appreciation

R is for reverence.
E is for everyone.
S is for special.
P is for person.
E is for esteem.
C is for courage.
T is for truth.

Work in groups

Think of situations at school, at home, in society or in the world when respect makes a difference.
Use the words of RESPECT above to help you.
Use at least one other resource: magazines, books, TV soaps, national or local newspapers.
Choose one of your examples and role play the situation.

Work as a class

◆ *Either:* add other words to the list above
  or: make your own poem, ballad or rap song to explain what leads to respect and why it is important.

Respect for others and self-respect cannot be separated. The respect and love shown to us helps us to develop a true sense of self-worth. Remember that 'worth' and 'worship' come from the same root.

Extension

◆ Look at your school mission statement. Evaluate how it values and invites respect.

Pause for thought

If you don't find God in the very next person you meet, it is a waste of time looking anywhere else.
(Mahatma Gandhi)

Check your learning ☑☑

Give one example from Scripture of when God chooses a person least expected for a huge responsibility. What did God see that others did not?

From good to evil

The Church teaches that God created a world in which all things were good. Human beings were made in God's image and given responsibility for creation. Yet sometimes it seems that everywhere there is misery, pain and suffering. Most of it is the result of the evil things that people do. Why?

Two-and-a-half-thousand years ago, the human authors of Genesis set out to explain how evil began. Their idea of paradise (heaven) was a beautiful garden. Their idea of evil was the back-breaking work of tilling the ground of the rocky desert lands where they lived. Life was uncertain and childbirth dangerous. God was the giver of life and the judge of human behaviour. The breakdown of the man and woman's relationship with God brought pain and suffering and the breakdown of their relationship with one another. This is named 'original sin' or, in other words, 'the origin of sin'.

Read Genesis 3:1–20.

Think and talk

The author uses images to tell his story.

1. What does the snake represent?
2. What does the tree symbolise?
3. What do the man and woman have?
4. Why are they not satisfied?
5. What do they think will make them happy?
6. What is their punishment?
7. What effect does this behaviour have on the world?
8. How might the outcome have been different?

West end window, St Mary the Virgin, Aylesbury: Adam and Eve and the Tree of Life, fifteenth century.

What's behind it all?

Five hundred years later Jesus was challenged by the Pharisees about what was sinful. They considered themselves the guardians of the law. They thought they kept it so faithfully that they had the right to *interpret* it for others. Jesus accused them of being hypocrites. They were faithful to outward details. Their interpretations were always favourable to themselves and often made life difficult for others. They were strict judges and seemed to forget God is a God of mercy and compassion.

Jesus encourages people to think about what sin really means. It is not just about keeping rules. It is also about what a person has in his or her heart.

interpret: to explain, to translate, to act as a go-between

Read Mark 7:20–23.

Classwork

A. *What do you think Jesus meant? List the sins Jesus names here. Think of different reasons why someone would do these things. Is there a common reason?*

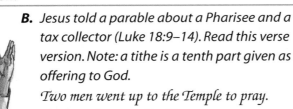

B. *Jesus told a parable about a Pharisee and a tax collector (Luke 18:9–14). Read this verse version. Note: a tithe is a tenth part given as offering to God.*

Two men went up to the Temple to pray.
Each spoke to God in his own way.
One stood apart and addressed the Lord:
"I'm not like that wretch over there, thank God!
I'm not greedy, dishonest or a cheat.
I fast two days of every week.
I keep the laws and my tithes are precise;
But that tax collector – he's not nice!"
The man he mocked in the Temple court,
He bowed his head and his prayer was short.
"Have mercy on me, Lord, I'm a sinner."
"D'you know," asked Jesus, "who was the winner?
The one who boasted didn't know his place.
The other went home in God's good grace."

C. *Who is the hero of the story? Explain.*

Pause for thought

Even in the best of hearts there remains a small corner of evil.
(Alexander Solzhenitsyn)

2D People of spirit and truth

Sin

Sin is a free choice of something that is against genuine love of God, of neighbour or oneself. Many times, over the centuries, the Church has returned to the question of how sin began, but above all, it reminds people when they read the story of Genesis to remember that Jesus is the One who saves the world from sin and brings the gift of new life. Sin is evidence of the struggle between good and evil. The Church recognises in the story of Genesis that sin is part of human life. Sin is a reality in human life and each person has to recognise his or her personal sin. The sacraments and liturgy offer opportunities to do this and, at the same time, invite everyone to trust in God's unchanging love, forgiveness and help.

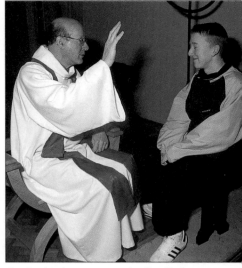

An invitation to trust in God's love.

At the beginning of the celebration of the Eucharist the Church prays for the forgiveness of sins. For example:

All:
I confess to almighty God,
and to you, my brothers and sisters,
that I have sinned through my own fault,
in my thoughts and in my words,
in what I have done,
and in what I have failed to do;
and I ask blessed Mary, ever virgin,
all the angels and saints,
and you, my brothers and sisters,
to pray for me to the Lord our God.

Priest:
May almighty God have mercy on us,
forgive us our sins,
and bring us to everlasting life.
Amen.

Think and talk

1. Re-read the 'I confess'.
2. Identify words or phrases that show that sin:

   is personal — damages relationship with God and with others

   affects others — has effects for life now and for ever

   is weakness — involves choices.

Pause for thought...

A crowded river ferry began to sink. Many passengers found places in the lifeboats, but some had to swim for the shore. From the bank they watched the ferry going down. Suddenly they saw a man come up on to the deck. He jumped for a floating piece of wreckage, missed and sank like a stone. Later, when his body was washed ashore, they found his pockets crammed with stolen property, and bags of gold and jewellery tied to his belt. He had spent his last moments ransacking the baggage of the other passengers. The weight of the ill-gotten goods had dragged him down.

Conscience

No one can commit a sin by accident. Sin is a free choice of something that is against genuine love of God, of neighbour or oneself.
But how do we know what is against the love of God, neighbour or self?
We rely on our *conscience* to guide us and help us first to judge what is right and wrong, and then make a decision.

Conscience is not just our feelings about what is or is not against the law of love. Feelings can change from day to day, and so they are not wholly reliable. In order to judge, conscience needs to be *informed*, to be guided by *objective* information and take all the steps needed.

Conscience makes a judgement by:
◆ following God's law of love
◆ knowing the Church's teaching
◆ listening to wise advice
◆ reflecting carefully, honestly and critically on one's feelings
◆ praying for the help of God the Holy Spirit.

conscience con = with
   science = knowledge – the power to judge with knowledge
informed properly informed; having the necessary information
objective not based on personal feelings
formation development, what helps something to develop, learning and training

When a person has done all this, his or her judgement can be made with an informed conscience.
Must a person follow his or her conscience? Yes.
Can the judgement a person makes be mistaken?
Yes, if he or she is ill-informed or does not take all the necessary steps.

The final, important step is to pray for the strength to take the decision that follows from your honest judgement.

Conscience is sometimes described as the voice of God in each human heart. Each baptised Christian has to take responsibility for the *formation* of his or her conscience. Parents take responsibility for their children until they are old enough to be responsible for themselves. Catholics believe that conscience is formed through:
– relationship with God in prayer
– listening to and reading God's Word
– studying and knowing the Church's teaching
– discussion and the advice of trusted people.

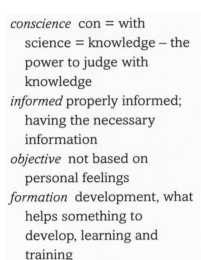

Homework 🏛

Tell a story about someone making a difficult moral choice. Include the steps they took to reach their decision. Explain carefully the place of conscience in the whole process that led them towards their decision.

2D People of spirit and truth

Links

Pause for thought

Dare to be true.
(George Herbert)

Test ?

1. How does the author of Genesis explain the origin of sin?

2. Where did Jesus say sin comes from?

3. What was the prayer of the publican?

4. What is conscience?

5. Name four ways in which a Catholic forms his or her conscience.

Faith alive

> Look around you, can you see?
> Times are troubled, people grieve.
> See the violence, feel the hardness;
> all my people, weep with me.
> *Kyrie eleison.*
> *Christe eleison.*
> *Kyrie eleison.*

'Look around you, can you see', Jodi Page Clark

Note: *Kyrie eleison* comes from the Greek. It means 'Lord have mercy'. *Christe eleison* means 'Christ have mercy'.

Key words

In your personal file write down the following words and a one-sentence explanation for each:

respect

conscience

sin

self-worth

Challenge

'If I'm not happy, why should you be?'

'If you've got something I want, why shouldn't I take it?'

'Who's going to tell me I'm wrong?'

Can you think of a sin that doesn't hurt yourself or others?

Churches together

People come together for many reasons. They can be united for positive and negative purposes.

In groups, discuss:
1. What is uniting the people in these photographs?
2. Will their coming together have positive or negative results?
3. Give examples of unity and division from your own experience as a class, year group or school community.

A
B
C 2/3 E
D
E

In this section of our work we will be learning:

◆ what unites and what divides people
◆ about different Christian Churches in England and Wales
◆ about the week of prayer for Christian Unity.

Words we use

unity – oneness, coming together, acting as a unit

division – separation into parts, for example, in Maths or a vote in Parliament
– part of a larger whole, for example, a military division is part of an army
– disagreement between groups or in a group

diversity – number or variety of anything, for example, nationalities in a school
– range of differences, for example, in dress styles or tastes in music

Copymasters ⑬ and ⑭ *What builds up? What knocks down?*

In Year 7 you learned that Christians who follow Jesus belong to different Churches. In this section of work you will be investigating what unites and divides them, and in Year 9 you will study the beginnings of division in the Church in England and Wales.

Check your learning ☑☑

Decide which of the following are Christian believers: Anglicans, Sunni, Methodists, Christian Scientists, Baptists, Gospel Singers, Buddhists.

Pause for thought

If we cannot end our differences, at least we can help make the world safe for diversity.
(John F Kennedy, USA President)

Project: The churches in our neighbourhood

Work as a class

1. Collect information about some different churches in your neighbourhood; for example, any that you pass on the way to school. Note the name of the church. Here are some to look out for: Catholic, Anglican, United Reformed.
2. Make a neighbourhood map of your findings.
3. Make a collection of information about each church from church notice boards, newsletters, parish magazines or newspapers, friends or neighbours.
4. Look for similarities and differences. For example, titles of clergy, days and times of services, names of services, feast days.
5. Prepare a questionnaire or letter to local churches. What questions will you ask? Who will write the letter or design the questionnaire?
   Or if possible, invite a member(s) of a local Christian church to talk with the class. Prepare your questions for the visitor. What kind of record of the information will you make?

Come worship the Lord

For all Christians, Sunday is the Lord's Day. In many places the ringing of church bells is a call to worship. Read the following descriptions of Sunday worship.

My name is Gillean and I belong to the Church of England, which is often also called the Anglican Church. My church is St James, and on St James' day in July we always have a big celebration and music and a party after the Service. There is a large choir of men and boys, some as young as six, who make beautiful music for the services.

I usually go to the Sung Eucharist at 10.30 on Sundays. We use one of the modern forms of service where we address God as 'You' rather than 'Thee'. There are usually three readings. We use the same readings as the Roman Catholics and Methodists. One comes from the Old Testament, one from the Letters in the New Testament and one from the Gospels. We stand for the reading from the Gospel to underline its

importance. After the readings we listen to a sermon preached by one of the clergy, who are all men, or by our trained lay minister, who is a woman.

Next the clergy go up to the altar, which is at the east end of the church and raised up so that everyone can see. Two members of the congregation take up bread and wine to symbolise the offering of our work and our lives to God. The priest says a special prayer over these offerings. This remembers the Last Supper when Jesus said that, when we eat this bread and drink this wine, he is with us and in us. The people come forward and kneel down to receive this special food and drink. The choir sing quietly and we try to be quiet and reverent towards God made present to us in this way.

My name is Pam and I worship in the Baptist Church in a small city.

Last Sunday I was welcomed at the door and shown to a pew. The organ was playing a classical piece of music. The service began when the Minister called us to worship. He wears an ordinary suit with a collar and tie. We sang from the hymn-book: 'Praise my soul, the King of Heaven'. In the congregation there were elderly people and some families with children. Upstairs in the gallery were some teenagers. The Minister led us in prayers and then the Associate Minister, a young woman, spoke to the children about Moses and how he led the children of Israel out of Egypt.

After that we made our offering, which the children helped to collect. Then the children left the church for their 'J Team' activities. Next the choir sang a modern song about Moses. Two members of the congregation read passages from the Bible. We sang another hymn and then the Senior Minister went into the pulpit to preach the sermon. It was about Moses and the journey in the desert. We sang another hymn before the Minister led us in prayers for the world. The service ended with another hymn and a blessing which we said to each other.

My name is Nick. I started going to Quaker meetings because a Friend invited me. The proper name for Quakers is The Society of Friends. I like their belief that we must seek for truth everywhere and in everyone. They say it means looking for the extraordinary in the ordinary and for 'that of God in everyone'.

I have been to 10 Meetings. That is the name for Quaker worship. It takes place in a simple room with the chairs in a circle. There are no statues, pulpit or altar. In the middle of the circle is a table. On it are three books: the Bible and two Quaker books: Christian Faith and Practice and Advices and Queries.

The meeting begins when the first person sits down in the room in silence. There may be over 100 people, or just five or six. Some meetings sit in complete silence for the hour, but usually two or three people speak. This is called vocal ministry. People read from the Bible or other books, talk about something that has happened, or share their thoughts. People will only speak if they feel strongly moved to do so and every contribution should be spontaneous. In silence we feel at one with the other people there and find new strength and love. The meeting for worship is a kind of communion but there is no priest, no hymns, no sharing bread and wine and no set sermon.

After about an hour the elders, who are responsible for the smooth running of the meeting for worship, shake hands as a sign that the meeting is over. The clerk reads the notices and then we have tea and coffee.

Classwork

A. Choose one example of Sunday worship and explain what would make you feel at home. What questions would you want to ask about what is different?

B. What is common in each act of worship? What is different?

C. Read Ephesians 4:1–6. In what ways could the Christian Churches of today put Paul's advice into practice in their Sunday worship?

May they all be one

John's gospel records a prayer of Jesus for his disciples:

*I pray not only for these, but also for those who, through
their teaching, will come to believe in me. May they all be
one, just as, Father, you are in me and I am in you, so that
they also may be in us, so that the world may believe it was
you who sent me. I have given them the glory you gave to
me, that they may be one as we are one. With me in them
and you in me, may they be so perfected in unity that the
world will recognise that it was you who sent me and that
you have loved them as you have loved me.*
(John 17:20–23)

"You are Peter, and upon this rock I will build my Church." (Matthew 16:18)

Unity is the gift of the Trinity, Father, Son and Holy
Spirit. The Church is united by its head, Jesus Christ,
and is made one by the Holy Spirit. Within this unity,
there is a diversity of peoples and cultures and a rich
variety of gifts, ministries and ways of life.
Jesus entrusted the unity of his Church to his apostles
with Peter as the leader, 'the rock' on which his
Church would stand firm. The Pope and bishops, as
successors of the apostles, safeguard this gift through
their faithfulness to the gospel and doctrine of the
Church, and by their unity as teachers and leaders.

From its beginning the Church has had to confront and
overcome quarrels and divisions. The Acts of the
Apostles and the letters of St Paul describe some of
these and how they were resolved.
Sometimes the disagreements were between
individuals. For example, Paul begs Evodia and
Synthche to end their quarrel (Philippians 4:2–3).

*Handing of the Keys to St Peter,
attributed to the Master of the Legend
of the Holy Priest, c 1470.*

Other situations meant the whole Church had to come
to an agreement about the way forward. One of the
first arguments was about the Gentiles, non-Jews, who
became Christians. Should they be circumcised according to
the Jewish law as well as baptised according to the Christian?
The apostles and elders met in Jerusalem to discuss the
matter and then wrote a letter that gave their decision (Acts
15–16:34).
This set a pattern for the future. These meetings of the
Church elders came to be called Councils. They would
decide questions of faith, law and general
Church business.

The sadness of division

For about the first 1,000 years of Christian history this worked fairly well. Then in 1054 came a disagreement that split the Church. The Church in the West, led by the Pope, the Bishop of Rome, and the Church in the East, led by the Patriarch of Constantinople, separated.

About 500 years later groups in Europe, including England, split away from the Catholic Church. The Christian family was divided and Christians persecuted one another. Christ's commandment to 'love one another' seemed forgotten.

For many people, the most painful result of this split is in the celebration of the Eucharist. This greatest of sacraments is the sign of the unity of Christ's Body. Those not in full membership, communion, in the Catholic Church join in the celebration of the Mass, but are not permitted to receive holy communion. The divisions in the Church that occurred in the sixteenth century, and some since then, are centred on teaching about the Eucharist and the sacrament of Holy Orders.

In spite of these divisions, the Catholic Church, together with other Christian Churches, works and prays for a new visible unity between all Churches. This is the desire and gift of Jesus Christ.

Group task

Look back to the accounts of Sunday worship by different Christians (pp. 64–65).

1. What evidence can you find of some of the divisions that split the Church? What do you think caused these?
2. Draw up a five-point action plan that you think would help the churches in your area to work together for unity.

Hope for unity

Today the Catholic Church offers its members a new image for appreciating the Church's unity. It invites them to think of a pilgrimage. All Christians are journeying towards God. All Christians are journeying towards unity. The movement towards Christian unity is called *ecumenism*. This comes from the Greek word meaning 'one inhabited world' or 'household'. All Christians have a responsibility to work for Christian Unity through prayer and dialogue.

In 1990 the Roman Catholic Church in England and Wales became a full member of the Churches Together in Britain and Ireland (CTBI). England and Wales also have their own groups: Churches Together in England (CTE) and Churches Together in Wales (CYTUN).

Pause for thought

Spirituality, social action and education are, for me, priorities which we can try to address together.

(Cardinal Basil Hume)

Pope Paul VI and Patriarch Athenagoras in the church of the Holy Sepulchre in 1964, the first meeting of a patriarch and a pope since the schism of 1054.

1. What can the Churches do together?
2. Research people who live Christian unity; the Iona Community in Scotland; Taizé, France; Corymeela, Northern Ireland.
3. Find out what happens in your local area. Create a class notice board: 'Churches together in ...'

A week of prayer

A special prayer effort for Christian Unity was the idea of a community of Episcopalian Christians in America. The founders were Father Lewis T Wattson and Mother Lurana Mary White. The community began at Graymoor, New York, in 1898. Their longing for unity led the whole community to enter into full communion with the Roman Catholic Church in 1909. They knew that not all Christians would do this, but they believed everyone could do something about unity. They began the Church Unity *Octave*. It is now a world-wide event, beginning on 18 January, the feast of St Peter's Chair, and ending on 25 January, the feast of the Conversion of St Paul. Recently some Churches in England and Wales have decided that Pentecost is a good time for prayer for Christian Unity.

Mother Lurana Mary White.

1. How does your school mark the Week of Prayer for Christian Unity?
2. Why is Pentecost a good time to pray for unity?
3. Hold your own week/day of work and prayer for Christian Unity. Plan a prayer service. Is there a way of inviting other Christian groups to join your prayer?

octave: eight days

A Catholic and an Anglican bishop meet in Christian Unity Week.

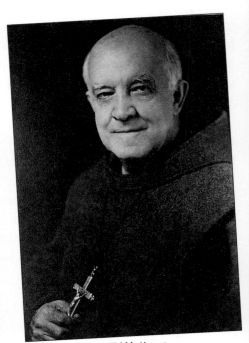

Father Lewis T Wattson.

Homework 🏛

Prepare a flyer to advertise a Prayer Service for Christian Unity for KS3 students. As well as practical information on time, place and so on, include some ideas about why Christian Unity is important for everyone. Choose an appropriate symbol.

Pause for thought 💭

In order to be united we must love one another; to love one another we must know one another; to know one another we must meet one another.

Links

Design a symbol for Christian Unity.

Test

1. *Name three different Christian Churches in your neighbourhood.*

2. *Who began the Week of Prayer for Christian Unity? When?*

3. *What image does the Catholic Church offer for Christian Unity?*

4. *Name two groups who work for Christian Unity.*

5. *What was Jesus' prayer for his Church?*

Key words

In your personal file write down the following words and a one-sentence explanation for each:

Christian Unity

ecumenism

diversity

division

dialogue

Challenge
Let there be peace and unity: and let it begin with me.

Faith alive

Renew in our own days your miracles
like a second Pentecost.
Grant that the Church,
reunited in prayer,
may extend the kingdom of Jesus:
a kingdom of truth and justice,
of love and peace. Amen.

(Prayer in preparation for the Second Vatican Council)

Pause for thought

In essential things – unity;
in unimportant things – freedom;
in all things – charity.
(Pope John XXIII)

Another step

Explain the obstacles and the hopes for Church unity as you see them today.

Other Faiths: Judaism

In your work this year you have learned about Jesus the Jew (1A) and the Covenant which Christians and Jews share (2A). In this section you are studying the Jewish faith community today.

The Catholic Church believes that God's revelation has come through the Jews; it calls its members to remember that Jesus was born of a Jewish mother and that the apostles and first disciples were Jews.

In this section of our work we will be learning:

◆ something about the story of the Jewish community in England and Wales
◆ about the Passover festival, the celebration of Jewish faith.

Check your learning

Work in a group.
Look at the photographs.
Choose the caption that fits each.
1. The Menorah: one of Judaism's oldest symbols.
2. The Sabbath meal.
3. A Torah Scroll.
Use what you know or have learned about Judaism to add one sentence to each caption.

Jews in Britain

Jews first settled in England in the eleventh century. They served primarily as money lenders and bankers for William the Conqueror. The Jews were guaranteed special privileges to provide a money-lending service.
There was racial unrest for many years. The most serious was at York in 1190. By 1290, Edward I found the Jews so poor that he expelled them from England. More than 16,000 Jews left the country.
It was not until 1565 that a bill was passed in Parliament to revoke the law of 1290 and permit Jews to live in England again.

Research the Jewish population in Britain. Find out where large Jewish communities live. If you can, visit your nearest synagogue. How is it arranged? What services are held? Who takes part? If you are unable to visit a synagogue, try to watch a video about a synagogue and use it to answer the same questions.

Extension

◆ *Either:* research the story of the Jews of York and the massacre of Clifford's Tower. What steps have been taken to heal this tragic injustice?
◆ *Or:* research the story of at least one Jewish person or family who came to Britain as survivors of the Holocaust, the Nazi systematic slaughter of all Jews during the Second World War.

Clifford's Tower, York.

The Festival of Freedom

Throughout the centuries, the great Jewish feast has been *Pesach*, Passover. It symbolises and re-enacts the Exodus from slavery in Egypt. It is a festival of freedom, a celebration that calls Jews to cherish freedom and liberty as basic requirements of life. The festival proclaims Jewish belief that liberty is the right of every human being as a child of God.

The *Seder* meal is the highlight of the festival. It is a family gathering. The father is the teacher and the children learn the lesson of freedom from every object on the table, from the food and from the prayers and songs.

Seder: Hebrew word for 'order'; every part of the meal and each food has its own place and significance.

Pesach: passover; the Angel of Death passed over the houses of the Israelites; the paschal lamb sacrificed on this day in the Temple
peh-sah, 'the mouth speaks': the words of the ritual re-enactment are the sacrifice today.

Work in groups

Use Copymaster 15 : ***The Seder Table***

  1 Choose two symbols.
  2 Discuss the experiences they symbolise.
  3 How would the people in the situation have felt?
  4 Why do you think their experience is remembered today?
  5 Make notes.
  6 Share your findings as a class.

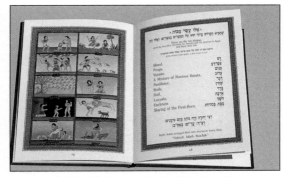

Haggadah is Hebrew for 'telling' – the story of Pesach.

=== Homework 🏛 ===

Use your notes to help you to think of your own symbols for the two experiences you discussed. In words or design, explain your symbol and why you have chosen it.

A key part of the Seder meal is telling the story of the Jewish people.
It is more than just recalling a memory. The *Haggadah* asks that in every generation people must think of themselves as the people who left Egypt. Believers must never forget that the task of seeking freedom for the oppressed is never ended. The story is told in actions and prayers.

Work as a class

Using the texts on pp. 72–73, read each section. Make notes of the actions and words.
Notice how different members of the family take part in the service.

One

Blessing the first cup of wine

Our story tells that in diverse ways, with different words, God gave promises of freedom to our people. With cups of wine we recall each one of them. (Exodus 6:6)

I am Yahweh and I will free you from the burdens of the Egyptians. I will deliver you from the bondage of the Egyptians. I will redeem you with an outstretched arm. And I will take you to be my people.

Karpas: rebirth and renewal

Eating of the Karpas symbolises the coming of Spring and the birth of the Jewish nation. Dipping herbs in salt water encourages children to ask why this is done and so the story of the Exodus will be told. A reading from the Song of Songs. 2: 10–12.

Ya'hatz: breaking of the matzah

Unleavened bread symbolises the slave bread which the Israelites made in Egypt when their time was not their own. It is also the bread of haste made when they had no time to let bread rise, but had to flee Egypt. The three matzah have several symbolic meanings: two are for the remaining days of the holiday. The third matzah is broken in half. One half is eaten and one half is hidden. This is called the *Afikomen*.

Two

Magid: telling the story of the Exodus

The central and longest part of the Seder. The youngest child asks the dramatic question:
Why is this night different from all other nights?
On all other nights, we eat either leavened bread or matzah; on this night only matzah.
On all other nights we eat all kinds of herbs;
on this night, we especially eat bitter herbs.
On all other nights, we do not dip herbs at all;
on this night we dip them twice.
On all other nights, we eat in an ordinary manner;
tonight we dine with special ceremony.

The whole story of God's saving actions is summed up in a song of praise.

Had God brought us out of Egypt and not divided the sea for us, Dayeinu!
Had God divided the sea and not permitted us to cross on dry land, Dayeinu!
Had God permitted us to cross the sea on dry land and not sustained us for forty years in the desert, Dayeinu!
Had God sustained us for forty years in the desert and not fed us with manna, Dayeinu!
Had God fed us with manna and not given us the Sabbath, Dayeinu!
Had God given us the Sabbath and not brought us to Mount Sinai, Dayeinu!
Had God brought us to Mount Sinai and not given us the Torah, Dayeinu!
Had God given us the Torah and not led us into the land of Israel, Dayeinu!
Had God led us into the land of Israel and not sent us prophets of truth, Dayeinu!
Had God sent us prophets of truth and not made us a holy people, Dayeinu!

The second cup of wine is blessed

Therefore, let us rejoice
At the wonder of our deliverance
From bondage to freedom,
From agony to joy,
From mourning to festivity,

From darkness to light,
From servitude to redemption.
Before God let us ever sing a new song.
(Psalms to sing: 113, 114.)

Three

Matzah and Maror and Shankbone

The father explains the symbolism of the paschal lamb, the unleavened bread and bitter herbs.
Note: observant Jews have strict rules about how foods are to be cooked and served.

The meal

The family meal is shared. The mother and older children will have helped prepare the meal and set the table. Jewish communities in different parts of the world have national dishes that are special for this festival.

The hunt for the Afikomen

The children lead the hunt. For them it is a game. The search is also a symbol that the Jewish people are waiting for their final redemption that is still hidden.

Conclusion

This privilege we share will ever be renewed.
Until God's plan is known in full,
God's highest blessing sealed: Peace! Peace for us! For everyone!
For all people, this is our hope:
Next year in Jerusalem!
Next year, may all be free!

Four

The Final Blessing, Hallel psalms, conclusion

The name of the Eternal be blessed from now unto eternity.
On this Festival of matzot, inspire us to goodness.
On this Day of liberation, make us a blessing.
On this festival of Pesach, preserve us in life.
All Merciful, rule over us forever.
Sustain us with honourable work.
May the One who blessed Abraham, Isaac, and Jacob bless this house, this table, and all assembled here; and so may all our loved ones share our blessing.
God will give strength unto our people.
God will bless all people with peace.
(The Hallel psalms: 115–118.)

Discuss

Why do you think this festival is so important for the Jewish people?

What do you think are the advantages of making the celebration part of a family meal?

Classwork ✍

A. *A Jewish visitor is coming to talk to you about the Seder meal. Prepare two questions that you would want to ask him or her. Explain why you should be given the chance to ask your questions.*

B. *Prepare a Seder handbook that would help either a 10-year-old Jewish child who will be asking the four questions for the very first time, or a visitor to the Seder meal.*

C. *Describe the significance of the Jewish Festival of Freedom in a story or poem.*

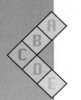

Links

Pause for thought

The home is the centre of the Jewish way of life.

Another step

Either: research one of the other Jewish festivals. When is it celebrated, how and why?

Or: research the events at Massadah. Why is this significant in the story of Jewish belief in freedom?

Present your findings in words, pictures, a video diary or a 15-minute radio programme.

Test ?

1. When did it become lawful for Jews to live in Britain?
2. What does 'Pesach' mean?
3. Name three symbolic foods used at a Seder meal.
4. Why is Pesach called the 'festival of freedom'?
5. What is the significance of the Cup of Elijah?

Challenge
What have I learned about Jews and Jewish faith?
What have I learned about the freedom I have or want?

Faith alive

God will give strength unto our people.
God will bless all people with peace.
(From the Final Blessing)

A place for everyone

Gifts for life

What gifts do you think would bring this child happiness and fulfilment? You may like to use some of the words below and find your own.

In this section of our work we will be learning:

◆ about the wonder of being human
◆ about Jesus' invitation to each person to live life to the full.

goodness	curiosity	sense of humour	love of justice
sense of adventure	truthfulness	generosity	kindness
courage	good health	friends	success
good luck	laughter	ability to trust	

What and who will help this child to develop these qualities?
What and who might prevent this child from achieving fulfilment?

Your task is to help this child to be happy. What would you choose as birthday gifts?
Think about what the child will need through the different stages of her life. For example, early childhood, adolescence. You may like to use some of these words and find your own.

support	money	challenges
success	obstacles	good friends
a good job	a good school	struggle
leisure	good teachers	illness
medical help	religion	holiday
failure	sports	prayer
contentment	romance	

In a group, compare your lists.
What do you agree about?
What is different? Why?

Unit 3 Here in this place

Awe, reverence and wonder

Some abilities seem to be essentially human. High on this list is the ability to be moved to laughter or tears, but many people would put the ability to wonder at the very top. Along with wonder go curiosity, awe and reverence. They are qualities that artists and scientists share.

Sir Bernard Lovell is a radio astronomer. During the Second World War he developed a radar system for bombers on night raids. After the war he played a key role in the development of Jodrell Bank, the astronomy experimental station. He was director there from 1951–81. An interviewer once asked him how he could reconcile his Christian faith with his expertise in science and technology. Carefully, Sir Bernard explained that science and technology are not the same. Science is part of the human search for meaning, the unrestricted desire to know. Technology harnesses some of that knowledge for good or ill. He described himself as a scientist whose journey to God was stimulated by the beauty of a graph.

Wonderfully made

There are about 100 million million cells in a human body, and the total area of membranous structure inside one of us works out at more than 200 acres. How many football pitches is that?

A message from an oyster

Look at it from my point of view. Think of how you can feel the tiniest stone in your shoe. Well, I have to start with a piece of grit inside my shell. Around it grows the protective covering that becomes the pearl. And you humans prize it so highly that you take my life. (We'll say nothing about what else of mine you prize, thank you.) What do you grow with the pieces of grit in your life?

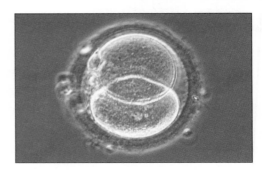

How would you answer the oyster's question?

Being Human

Talk about the following statements and decide how far they are true:
'Problems help you to grow.'
'Life needs both sunshine and storm.'

Pause for thought

God has created me to do him some definite service. He has committed some work to me which he has not committed to another.
(John Henry Newman)

Check your learning ✓✓

What does the book of Genesis say is unique about human beings?
What is a 'vocation'?

Life to the full

John's gospel has a number of short sentences in which Jesus describes himself and his mission. One of these is "I have come in order that you might have life – life in all its fullness." For Christians this means life in communion with Jesus and, through him, with God his Father by the power of the Holy Spirit. It means recognising life as God's gift. It means trusting that God has a loving plan for each person. It means trusting God's *grace* will be strength for action in life. It means trusting that God's purpose and plan for creation and for each person is *blessing*. All this leads to what the Scriptures call *'blessedness'*.

In the life of the Church, men and women of every nation, different ages, occupations and social situations are examples of 'fullness of life'. In 3D you will study this in more detail. Now you will study a passage from Mark's gospel that illustrates Jesus' invitation to 'fullness of life'.

grace: the touch of God's love in our lives; the gift of God's life in Jesus and through the sacraments

blessing: God's life-giving words and actions

blessedness: life with God; life in communion with God

Work in groups

Read Mark 10:17–22.
How are all the aspects of being human present in this story?

- the need to search and dream
- freedom and the power to choose
- the need for relationship
- the need for truth.

The following questions may help you.

1. What kind of person is the young man?
2. What does he want?
3. What does Jesus see in him?
4. How does Jesus act towards him?
5. How does Jesus challenge him?
6. What holds the young man back from accepting the challenge?
7. How does he feel? How does Jesus feel?
8. What do you think happened next in the life of the young man?
9. Would he have been able to forget Jesus' words? Why or why not?
10. Do you think he might come back?

 ## Homework

Continue the story in words – a story or play – in images, music or some other medium.

Pause for thought

The glory of God is the human person fully alive. Human life is the vision of God. God sleeps in a stone, dreams in a flower, moves in an animal and wakes in man.

St Irenaeus wrote this in the second century. What meaning do his words have for the world today?

Words we use

paradox – a statement or situation that appears a total contradiction, for example, 'the child is father of the man', meaning the kind of child you are shapes the kind of adult you will be

mystery – a puzzle to be solved, as in a murder mystery
– making present, active and known the wonderful life of God

eternal – for ever, everlasting, having no end; heaven is 'for ever life'

The Church believes that some aspects of 'fullness of life' can only be interpreted in the light of faith. One of these is that Jesus' death was a unique life-giving action. His death sets all creation free *from* sin and his resurrection sets all free *for* life with God for ever.

Jesus explained this paradox with an image:
"A grain of wheat remains no more than a single grain unless it is dropped into the ground and dies. If it does die it produces many grains." (John 12:24)

It is the next sentence that sums up the mystery of 'fullness of life'.

"Whoever loves his life will lose it; whoever hates his own life in this world will keep it for life eternal. Whoever wants to serve me must follow me." (John 12:25)

Jesus made it clear what following him meant. He had told his disciples that he would die on the cross. Mark's gospel adds this:

"If anyone wants to be a follower of mine, let him forget self and take up his cross and follow me." (Mark 8:34)

Think and talk

◆ What is the opposite of 'forget self'?
◆ Compare ideas of ways in which people have to 'forget self'.
◆ What did the cross mean for Jesus?
◆ What does 'cross' mean here?
◆ Brainstorm examples of what might seem a 'cross' for people of different ages and in different situations.
◆ Brainstorm other images that express 'death' leading to life.

☰ Classwork ☰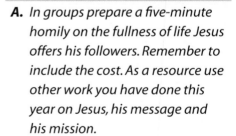

A. *In groups prepare a five-minute homily on the fullness of life Jesus offers his followers. Remember to include the cost. As a resource use other work you have done this year on Jesus, his message and his mission.*

The cost of discipleship

Fullness of life and the cross cannot be separated. Many disciples have found out what this means when life turned into a nightmare.

Dietrich Bonhoeffer (born 4 February 1906) was a theology lecturer in Berlin at the time of the Second World War. His opposition to Hitler led to his arrest in April 1943. He was sent to a concentration camp and died there on 9 April 1945.

In *The Cost of Discipleship* he wrote:
Cheap grace is grace without discipleship, grace without the cross, grace without Jesus Christ, living and incarnate. Costly grace is the treasure hidden in the field; for the sake of it a man will gladly go and sell all that he has. It is costly because it costs a man his life, and it is grace because it gives the only true life.

Maximilian Kolbe was a Polish priest. He wanted to use his talents as a journalist to spread the gospel, but his efforts were misunderstood and failed. During the Nazi occupation of Poland his boldness in speaking out for human rights led to his arrest. He was sent to the concentration camp at Auschwitz. One evening, the guards were choosing prisoners to die of starvation as a punishment. One of those chosen pleaded for his life. Maximilian volunteered to take his place. The small group were locked away in an underground bunker. Father Maximilian was the last to die. Forty-one years later, on 10 October 1982, Maximilian Kolbe was canonised. The man whose place he had taken was present at the ceremony.

Edith Stein was 15 when she decided she did not believe in God and stopped praying. A year later she wrote in her diary, 'a serious search for truth had begun'. Twelve years later she wrote, 'I read the life of St Teresa of Avila and my unbelief collapsed'. She was baptised a Catholic on 1 January 1922. Edith had a promising future as philosopher, writer and university lecturer, but in 1933 she was told she could not teach because she was a Jewess. She entered the Carmelites and was sent to Holland where she continued her writing and offered her life to God for peace in her native land. On 26 July 1942 the Dutch bishops issued a pastoral letter on Racism and Anti-Semitism. The next day the Nazis ordered the deportation of Jews. Edith was arrested and deported to Auschwitz. On 9 August she became one of the millions who died in the gas chambers. In 1987 she was beatified as a martyr by Pope John Paul, who proclaimed St Teresa Benedicta of the Cross (Edith Stein) Co-patroness of Europe.

Classwork

B. Choose one of these people or someone like them. Research the ways in which they had fullness of life in spite of, or because of, what happened to them.
You will need to find out: when and where they lived; what they did; how they found themselves in a difficult situation; how they coped; what helped them to cope; what their experiences meant to them. Prepare a display for a school notice board: 'People of Courage'.

C. Write a poem or paragraph that could be used for a 'Thought for the Day' on a school retreat or day of prayer. You want people to think about the paradox of Christian life.

Links

Pause for thought

Life is a miracle that happens every day.

Faith alive

*Unless a grain of wheat shall fall upon the ground and die,
It remains but a single grain with no life.*

*If we have died with him then we shall live with him:
if we hold firm we shall reign with him.*

*Make your home in me as I make mine in you:
Those who remain in me bear much fruit.*

*Peace I leave with you, my peace I give to you:
Peace which the world cannot give is my gift.*

'Unless a Grain of Wheat', Bernadette Farrell

How might these promises of Jesus have
comforted and strengthened Maximilian Kolbe,
or any of the other disciples you researched?

Challenge
If you would be a follower
of mine, take up your cross
and follow me.

Test ?

1. Quote the sentence from John's
   gospel that speaks of life to the full.
2. What question did the rich young
   man ask Jesus?
3. What did Jesus' reply mean?
4. What is a paradox?
5. Explain 'unless a grain of wheat dies,
   it remains but a single grain'.

A sacred place

A task worthy of God

Elzéard Bouffier was a man of extraordinary commitment and generosity. At the beginning of the twentieth century he transformed a barren, lifeless region into a fruitful homeland for thousands of people. Jean Giorno tells the story in the book *The Man Who Planted Trees*.

> **In this section of our work we will be learning:**
> ◆ about how people show respect and care for the world
> ◆ about the Church's belief that people are called to work with God in caring for the world.

After the tragic loss of his son and his wife, Elzéard went to live alone as a shepherd. He saw that the land was dying for lack of trees and he set out to do something about it. Each evening he would carefully select sound acorns, examining each one individually. Each day he would plant these on the barren hills. The traveller who told his story learned that in three years Elzéard had planted 100,000 acorns. Of these, 20,000 had sprouted, and he reckoned that about half would survive. When he found that his sheep were damaging the young trees he became a beekeeper instead and cared for 100 hives. As well as oaks he planted beech trees and birches in the dales. The area he transformed was some 11 kilometres long and three kilometres wide. He began his work before the First World War and worked through that war and the Second World War. He worked alone until he died in 1947 at the age of 87. The trees he planted restored the earth's natural cycle and streams and rivers flowed again. Birds and wildlife returned. People came to wonder at the phenomenon of a natural forest. In an area where scattered inhabitants had fought one another in an effort to gain a living, deserted villages were rebuilt. Soon there were settlers in farms and villages sharing the richness of the land. Elzéard's patience and generosity of spirit had accomplished a task worthy of God.

(You can discover the full story from the book or video *The Man Who Planted Trees*.)

Discuss

1. What led Elzéard to begin his work of planting trees?
2. What qualities helped him to see it through?
3. Why did people think the forest had grown naturally?
4. What were the results of his work and who benefited from it?

Pause for thought

Recycle, reuse, reduce.

Classwork

1. *Make a list of the kinds of food you eat, types of entertainment you enjoy, your use of nature's resources, clothes you wear. What changes could you make in your lifestyle that would help the environment rather than harm it? List five examples.*

2. *Write to a large international/multi-national company asking them for their views about protecting the environment. Display their responses.*

3. *Carry out a survey in your school to see how much paper is wasted. Mount a display to show your findings to the school. Don't forget areas like kitchens and staff room.*

Co-creators

The Scriptures make it clear that God is the Creator and people are called to work with God in caring for the earth. The earth and all its riches are a gift from God. Everyone is called to be actively responsible for God's gift. This means being a 'co-creator', sharing God's work of creation.

From the Book of Genesis

God created humankind in his image, in the image of God he created them: male and female he created them. God blessed them, and God said to them, "Be fruitful and multiply, and fill the earth and subdue *it; and* have dominion *over the fish of the sea and the birds of the air and over every living thing that moves upon the earth." God said, "See, I have given you every plant yielding seed that is upon the face of all the earth, and every tree with seed in its fruit; you shall have them for food."* (Genesis 1:27–30)

Think and talk

Now look up:
Genesis 1:1–31 or Isaiah 40:12–22 (the environment we live in)
Deuteronomy 22:6, Matthew 6:26–30 or Job 12:7–10 (animal life)
Ephesians 2:10 or 1 John 4:7–11 (human life).
1. Explain in your own words what each passage is saying.
2. What is the Bible's message about care and respect for the environment?

Getting the message

Use the reading from Genesis and evidence from news media to decide which of the following show people acting as responsible or irresponsible co-creators:

sea defences	culling
breeding	genetic engineering
conservation	protection of species
game parks	zoos
battery farming	land clearing
hunting	mining.

Pause for thought

Wow! Sometimes the only thing to do is to stand in awe!
To be is a blessing, to live is holy.

Check your learning ✓✓

1. Which book of the Bible tells the story of the creation of the world?
2. What is its message about God and about creation?

subdue: control, keep in order, hold back

have dominion: have power over, be in charge of, be responsible for

The Christian heritage

The Church believes that Creation reflects God the Creator. God speaks through Creation. In the natural things – fire, water, seed and fruit – we can read the signs of God.

Read and study these examples of how Christian tradition shows God as Creator and creation as God's gift, reflecting the Creator.

St Patrick was asked to explain his religion to two pagan princesses. They were Celts who worshipped nature gods in trees and fields and springs. They wanted to know where they could find the God Patrick worshipped. The text below is part of his answer:

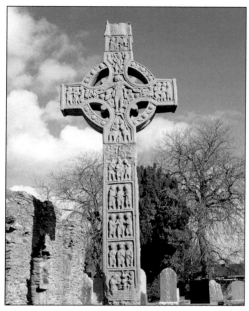

The cross of Christ is at the heart of the circle of the world. The carvings tell the story of God at work in the history of humankind and how men and women co-operated or not.

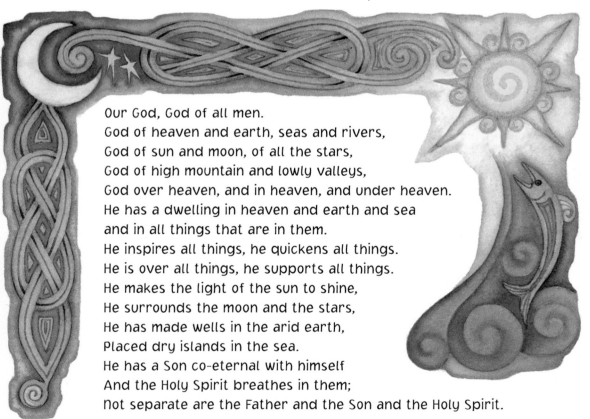

Our God, God of all men.
God of heaven and earth, seas and rivers,
God of sun and moon, of all the stars,
God of high mountain and lowly valleys,
God over heaven, and in heaven, and under heaven.
He has a dwelling in heaven and earth and sea
and in all things that are in them.
He inspires all things, he quickens all things.
He is over all things, he supports all things.
He makes the light of the sun to shine,
He surrounds the moon and the stars,
He has made wells in the arid earth,
Placed dry islands in the sea.
He has a Son co-eternal with himself
And the Holy Spirit breathes in them;
Not separate are the Father and the Son and the Holy Spirit.

You may know part of Patrick's words as the prayer called St Patrick's Breastplate. It is also a popular hymn.

3B A sacred place

God ever present

Awareness of the presence of God is part of the Christian tradition of these islands. The Celts and Anglo-Saxons found images for their prayer all around them and in everything they did. God the Father, Son and Holy Spirit were ever present. Everything that was part of creation and human life was under God's care.

A seventh-century prayer:
Pilgrim, remember,
For all your pain,
The Master you seek abroad
You will find at home –
Or walk in vain.

From the writings of Julian of Norwich, in a modern translation (*Meditations with Julian of Norwich*):

There is a treasure in the earth that is a food tasty and pleasing to the Lord.
Be a gardener.
Dig and ditch, toil and sweat, and turn the earth upside down,
and seek the dampness and water the plants in time.
Continue this labour and make sweet floods to run
and noble and abundant fruits to spring.
Take this food and drink
and carry it to God as your true worship.

Also from Julian:

I saw that God is everything that is good and energising.
God is our clothing
that wraps, clasps and encloses us
so as never to leave us.
God showed me in my palm,
a little thing round as a ball,
about the size of a hazelnut.
I looked at it with the eye of my understanding
and asked myself: "What is this thing?"
And I was answered: "It is everything that is created."
I wondered how it could survive, since
it seemed so little it could suddenly disintegrate into nothing.
The answer came: "It endures and ever will endure, because God loves it."
And so everything has being because of God's love.

In groups: talk about what you have read and studied

1. What have you learned about the Christian attitude to (a) God the Creator? (b) creation?
2. Present your answers as a set of slogans that could be used in a campaign about care for the environment.
3. Plan and run a campaign: 'Our school: a special place'.

You will need art skills to design posters. You will need to organise your campaign. Will you have a special assembly? Will you have a special liturgy? Will you have a Mass/prayer service outside? Will you involve the local community in your campaign?

Copymasters 16 and 17 : *Christian heritage* and *Handle with care*

Homework 🏛

1. Write your own prayer or poem in praise of the whole of creation. Or: design an icon, as a focus for prayer. Give your icon a title.

2. Collect a range of pictures, coloured and black and white, that show the many uses and links humans have with their environment. These should represent 'good', 'bad' and 'mixed' images.

Covenant with creation

Read Psalm 104.

Now read this covenant with creation:

We covenant today with one another:
– with every living creature and all on which we depend;
– with all that is on earth and with the earth itself;
– with all that lives in the waters and with the waters themselves;
– with all creatures of the air and with the air itself;
– with all that is warm with life, and with the living fire of God's Spirit.
We commit ourselves today to put away all selfishness and greed and to embrace one another and all creation in joy and peace.
(The Grail)

Classwork ✍

A. Identify words and phrases from these texts that tell you why people should care for creation. Choose two and explain them.

B. You are setting up a group to safeguard some aspect of your local environment. (For example, parks, canal, pedestrian or cycle paths.) Write your own covenant.

C. Write a letter you might send with your covenant to a friend or friends inviting them to commit themselves to it. Explain why they should do this.

Pause for thought 💭

The world's present and future depend on the safeguarding of Creation, because of the endless interdependence between human beings and their environment.
(Pope John Paul II, World Peace Day 1999)

3B A sacred place

Test

1. *List two ways in which people show care for the earth.*
2. *Identify two ways in which creation is misused.*
3. *Why do Christians believe that creation should be treated with reverence?*
4. *Choose something from your study of Christian tradition and explain its message about care for creation.*
5. *Write a definition of 'co-creator' and give an example of how someone can be a co-creator.*

In your personal file write down the following words and a one-sentence explanation for each:

Creator

creation

wonder

awe

reverence

Pause for thought

Care for creation and respect for people go together.

Challenge
How can you buy or sell the sky, the warmth of the land?
The earth does not belong to us: we belong to the earth.
Preserve the land for all children and love it as God loves us all.
(From *The Great Chief Sends Word*, Chief Seathl's testament, Edition published by Mount Saint Bernard Abbey, England)

Faith alive

The glory of the Lord shines through all his creation; nothing he has fashioned but hangs on his word.
(Ecclesiastes 42:15–16)

Another step

A Jewish story emphasises the importance of protecting the environment.

Our ancestor Abraham inherited his passion for nature from Adam. The later Rabbis never forgot it. Some twenty centuries ago they told the story of two men who were out on the water in a rowing boat. Suddenly, one of them started to saw under his feet. He maintained that it was his right to do whatever he wished with the place that belonged to him. The other answered that they were in the rowing boat together; the hole that he was making would sink both of them.

We are all passengers together in this same fragile and glorious world. Let us safeguard our rowing boats and let us row together.

Write a slogan for a cartoon that would give this message. Draw the cartoon if you want.

A place of hopes and dreams

In this section of our work we will be learning:
◆ about the kind of world people would like to live in
◆ how Jesus used parables to teach people about the Kingdom of God.

Does everyone have a dream?

Martin Luther King was a civil rights leader in America. He worked to improve the way of life for the people of the black community who were treated as second-class citizens. This is part of a speech that he gave in 1963:

"I have a dream that one day this nation will rise up and live the true meaning of its creed: 'We hold these truths to be self-evident: that we are all created equal.'
I have a dream that injustice and oppression will be transformed into freedom and justice.
I have a dream that one day my children will not be judged by the colour of their skin but by the content of their character.
I have a dream that black and white boys and girls will be able to join hands together as brothers and sisters.
When we let freedom ring, we will be able to speed up that day when all of God's children, black and white, Jews and Gentiles, Protestants and Catholics, will be able to join hands and sing in the words of the old Negro spiritual, 'Free at last! Free at last! Thank God Almighty, we are free at last!'"

Martin Luther King had a dream for a better world and worked hard trying to create it. He was assassinated for his beliefs in 1968.

Think and talk

1. What would make our world a better place today? List five points.
2. In your own words, explain Martin Luther King's dream.
3. Imagine that you have been asked to give a one-minute speech to the United Nations. Compose your own 'I have a dream' speech about your hopes for a better world today.
4. In groups, share your speeches.
5. As a class develop a 'Charter for true happiness' in your school community.

Reasons for living and hoping

Think about your reasons for living and hoping.

1. Share your views in words, pictures, music or song.
2. Write a short paragraph about someone whom you think gives others reasons for living and hoping. Explain the reasons for your choice.
3. Share your ideas.

Check your learning

What were some of the hopes and dreams of the Jewish people at the time of Jesus?

A greater hope

The crowds who came to Jesus were full of hope and expectation. They longed for a better world. Jesus was the greatest teacher. He understood them, heard them and offered them more than they could imagine. He used parables to do this.

A parable:
◆ uses the everyday things of life to focus its message
◆ challenges listeners to find the extraordinary in the ordinary
◆ surprises listeners
◆ invites a response.

Classwork

A. *In groups choose two or three of these parables.*

a mustard seed	*Matthew 13: 31–32*
a treasure and a pearl	*Matthew 13: 44–46*
a dragnet	*Matthew 13: 47–50*
yeast	*Matthew 13: 33*

Using the description of a parable given above, identify:

(a) *what is the everyday focus*

(b) *what is the extraordinary*

(c) *what is the message*

(d) *what is surprising*

(e) *what might the responses be.*

Present your findings in a visual display for the class.

Jesus' parables are about the Kingdom of God. He presented a Kingdom that was not a geographical area but about living in a close relationship with God. He invited people to open their eyes and ears to recognise the Kingdom. He invited them to open their hearts to God's rule, that is to say, a way of living guided by God's law. The parables do not offer a 'cosy' hope, but deal with the darkness and failure of human experience. Luke's gospel has a parable about God's invitation to a close relationship and the different responses people make.

Classwork

B. *Read Luke 14:15–24.*

1. *What images does Jesus use to describe the relationship with God?*
2. *Why do the invited guests not come?*
3. *What do their excuses tell us about them?*
4. *Who do you think they represent?*
5. *Who is then invited?*
6. *What is the parable's message about the Kingdom of God?*
7. *What picture of the Kingdom of God is given by this parable?*
8. *Why would the ending have surprised Jesus' listeners?*

C. *Why do you think Luke often uses 'banquet/feast' imagery for the Kingdom? In today's world how might people describe their discovery of the Kingdom?*

Pause for thought

The Kingdom of God is Justice, Love and Peace.

Think and talk

Which of the following are true of Jesus' teaching about the Kingdom?

◆ The kingdom is here and now.
◆ The kingdom is for Catholics only.
◆ The kingdom is about God being in charge.
◆ The kingdom is God coming close.
◆ The kingdom is a special welcome for the poor and sick.
◆ The kingdom is a place in the sky.
◆ The kingdom is about a way of living as a follower of Jesus.
◆ The kingdom is a set of rules and regulations.
◆ The kingdom will never end.
◆ The kingdom is described in Jesus' parables.
◆ The kingdom is also about life and death.

Discuss your response with others in a group.
Did you agree on everything?
Where did you differ? Why?

Words we use

Kingdom – God who comes close bringing light, healing, new life, judgement
Judgement – showing the darkness that needs God's light

Extension

Write a parable for today, for those who hope and dream.

3C A place of hopes and dreams

The Parable of the Sower

This is a well-known parable. The Sower is sowing God's message and the types of ground are the different types of people.

Seed on the path: people who, as soon as they hear God's message, allow it to be taken away from them by the devil.

Seed on the rocky ground: people who do not allow God's message to sink in, and who give up as soon as trouble comes their way.

Seed among the thorn bushes: people who are enthusiastic to start with, but soon get taken up with their own worries and the message is choked.

Seed sown in good soil: people who accept the message and allow it to grow within them so it begins to bear 'fruit'.

In groups

Prepare a modern-day drama of the Parable of the Sower and present it to the rest of the class.

Make notes of the other group presentations.

══ Homework 🏛 ══

Write an assessment of the group presentations of the Parable of the Sower. Use the following criteria to help you.

(a) The main message of the parable was clear.

(b) The updating was appropriate.

(c) The language made sense and was spoken well.

(d) All members of the group participated.

(e) The presentation caught and held the attention of the audience.

(f) The audience enjoyed the presentation.

Extension

Using art work, draw a symbolic picture of what the Kingdom of God is like. Use some of the imagery that Jesus used in his parables.

Links

Pause for thought

*Every parable is a story about God and a challenge to see the
Kingdom everywhere.*

Test ❓

1. What is the meaning of 'the Kingdom of God'?
2. What is a parable?
3. Name two parables that describe the Kingdom of God.
4. What is the meaning of the parable of the Sower?
5. Why did Jesus use imagery to get his message across?

Challenge
Thy kingdom come on earth as it is in heaven.

Another Step

Christ looked at the people.
He saw them assailed by fear:
He saw the locked door;
He saw the knife in the hand;
He saw the buried coin;
He saw the unworn coat, consumed by moth;
He saw the stagnant water drawn and kept in
the pitcher,
the musty bread in the bin –
the undefended, the unshared, the ungiven.
He told them then
of the love that casts out fear,
of the love that is four walls
and a roof over the head:
of the knife in the sheath,
of the coin in the open hand,
of the coin given
warm with the giver's life,
of the water poured in the cup,
of the table spread –
the defended, the shared, the given –
the Kingdom of Heaven.

Caryll Houselander, 'The Sermon on the
Mount' in *The Flowering Tree*.

Key *words*

In your personal file
write down the
following words and a
one-sentence
explanation for each:

Kingdom of God

vision

ideals

parables

symbolic picture

imagery

How many parables can you
recognise?
How does Caryll Houselander's poem
challenge her readers?

Faith alive

*The dream I have today, my Lord,
is only a shadow of your dreams for me;
only a shadow of all that will be,
if I but follow you.
My life is in your hands;
my life is in your hands.
My love for you will grow, my God.
Your light in me will shine.*

'Only a Shadow', Carey Landry

3C A place of hopes and dreams

3D ▶ A place for saints

My name is ...

"I'm named after my grandmother. She was a really strong person. My grandad died when my mum was only two and she brought her and my uncle and aunt up on her own. They never had much money but she always made sure they had enough to eat and had clothes for school. They even managed to have some family

holidays! My mum says she had a brilliant childhood. My grandmother died last year and we were all really sad. It's strange, but one of the things that comforted me a lot is that her name at least will live on in me. When I was younger, other kids at school sometimes laughed at the name Josephine when it was called out in the register. Sometimes I got upset but now I wouldn't because I'm really proud of my Christian name – especially when I think about how I got it."

Do you think Josie is right to be proud of her name? Why?

1. Find out what your name means.
2. As a group put together a Top Ten of the most popular boys' and girls' names in your year group or your school. See if you can find out how fashions in names change. For example, look at older family or friends, old school lists.

Cardinal Basil Hume was a great leader of the Catholic Church in England and Wales. He died in 1999. Shortly after he became Cardinal he was asked by someone who knew him quite well what he should now call him. (The correct official title for a Cardinal is 'Your Eminence' but this person had been used to calling him 'Father', as you would any priest.) Cardinal Hume replied that he could cope with most things but would not like to be called 'Oi You!'

Why do you think he said this?
Discuss your answer with others and think about what they say.

> ### In this section of our work we will be learning:
>
> ◆ why it is so important to be known by name
> ◆ why the Church names 'saints' and what it means to be a 'saint'
> ◆ what it means to call the Church 'the communion of saints'.

Christian names

Christians are baptised by name. Traditionally names are taken from the Old or New Testament or are of a person who has been important in the life of the Church. They are called Christian names because baptism is also called 'christening'. Today there are all kinds of Christian names. Some of them are based on what Christians believe in, for example, peace and hope. Any name can make a good Christian name as long as it reflects Christian belief and tradition.

1. Which of the following would be appropriate Christian names:

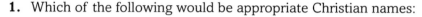

Peter   Mary   Anger   Sky   Bernadette   Paula
Mike   Hate   River   Coral   Jade   Whitney   Rose

2. For each of the ones you have chosen, say why it would make a good Christian name.

3. Imagine that in 15 years' time you had the chance to name your own baby. What name would you choose? Give your reasons. Share your answers.

Christian names can reflect the multi-cultural, multi-ethnic character of the universal Church. For example, both these names mean 'grace': Luse is from Zambia; Grainne is from Ireland.

Check your learning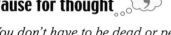

1. Write, in about 10 words, what the word 'saint' means to you.

2. See how many saints you can name.

All saints!

Saints are signs of God. They are men and women who are an example to others. They are signs of God's grace at work. Their holiness is a witness to God's blessing.

Saints come from all over the world. They show how Christianity has spread all over the globe. The name given to the way the Catholic Church makes someone a saint is 'canonisation'.

Saints are with God. They can and do intercede for people now. Some are better known than others: Saints Peter and Paul are very well-known and have their own feast day on 29 June each year. A feast day is a day when the Church remembers a particular saint.

Pause for thought

You don't have to be dead or perfect to be a saint. The struggle to be what God calls us to be is holiness.

The first of November is set aside each year as 'All Saints' Day'. The Church remembers and celebrates the millions of saints, including the unnamed, unknown and uncanonised men and women who have loved God and been faithful to God's commandments.

Mary, the Mother of Jesus, is especially honoured because of her openness to God's call and because of her unique role in the life of Jesus. Jesus is both God and man and the Church honours Mary as the Mother of God. She is addressed as 'Our Lady'. The Church celebrates several feast days in her honour.

Saints alive

When the Church names someone a saint, canonises him or her, it is accepting that the person has lived the gospel and is 'in heaven', alive in God. Today it usually takes a long time for the Church fully to recognise someone as a canonised saint. In the early centuries saints were named by popular acclaim, and still today people not yet officially canonised are recognised as holy because they were witnesses to the Gospel.

Oscar Romero.

Archbishop Oscar Romero

Archbishop Romero lived in El Salvador in central America. He often spoke out against the Government and was always being warned to keep his views to himself. Romero believed that his job as Archbishop meant he had to make sure that Christian teaching about fair treatment for the poor was heard. He was shot whilst saying Mass in 1980.

In 1998 five niches above the main entrance of Westminster Abbey were filled with modern-day witnesses:

Maximillian Kolbe, Catholic priest   Dietrich Bonhoeffer, Lutheran minister
Martin Luther King, Baptist minister   Oscar Romero, Catholic archbishop.
Janani Luwum, Anglican archbishop

Think and talk

Can you think of any people who have died recently or are alive today whom you think of as living saints? They don't have to be famous. They may be someone you think of as close to being the kind of person God wants them to be. Perhaps it will be someone who is a good example of what you think being a Christian is all about.

≡ Homework 🏛 ≡

You have the chance to write a letter to the Pope to suggest someone who should be canonised. Who will you choose and why?

Communion of saints? Does that mean us?

It certainly does!

The Communion of Saints

The Catholic Church believes in 'the Communion of Saints'.

This means that the members of the Church are united and made one by:

◆ faith in God as the Giver of Life to each person

◆ Jesus, through the sacraments, especially the Eucharist

◆ the Holy Spirit, through the gifts of the Spirit

◆ love, in response to the commandment to love God and one's neighbour.

The Communion of Saints celebrates all the saints, God's holy people, alive in one Body: those who are alive in this world and those who are with God in the next.

Patron saints

Organisations often choose a patron saint. This means that the organisation, the school or hospital or whatever it is, hopes that he or she will be a good example for everyone involved and pray for its success.

Countries also have patron saints. There are patron saints for jobs, crafts and a huge variety of human situations. For example, St Cecilia is the patron saint of musicians. St Jude is the patron saint of lost causes.

Think and talk

As a class, brainstorm organisations named after saints.

Why do you think they choose these names?

Is there always a Christian connection?

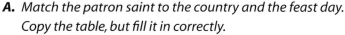

Classwork

A. *Match the patron saint to the country and the feast day. Copy the table, but fill it in correctly.*

Saint	Country	Feast Day
St George	Scotland	11 July
St David	Europe	17 March
St Patrick	England	23 April
St Andrew	Wales	1 March
St Benedict	Ireland	30 November

Add the patron saints of other countries that are important for people in the class.

Are there any special celebrations associated with these saints?

B. *Research the patron saint of your school, your diocese, your sport or hobby. Consult some of the following to help you: a dictionary of saints, a liturgical calendar (parish church or Internet), diocesan year book. Use these headings to present your findings:*

– *Saint's name*

– *The world of the saint*

– *What kind of person he or she was*

– *Why the Church celebrates this person's life and work.*

C. *Choose one saint from the past. What do you think he or she might be able to teach the Church today?*

3D A place for saints

Links

Go further

Compile your own class calendar of saints. This can include those already 'officially' known as saints by the Church. It can also include those whom you hope will be saints one day and those whom, although it is unlikely, you would like to become saints. Will you include yourselves?

Test ?

1. When is the Feast of All Saints celebrated in the Catholic Church?
2. Who are the patron saints of Ireland, Scotland, Wales and England?
3. Why was Archbishop Oscar Romero killed?
4. Explain the 'Communion of Saints'.
5. Name two ways in which saints are helpful to Christians today.

Pause for thought

If you were to be made a saint, of what or whom would you choose to be patron?

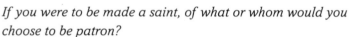

Challenge
Saints dead or alive: what's the point?

Faith alive

Oh when the Saints
Go marching in,
Oh when the Saints go marching in,
I want to be in that number
Oh when the saints go marching in.

Oh when the drums begin to beat …
Oh when the saints begin to shout …
Oh when the bands begin to play …
Oh when the choirs begin to sing …

Add your own verses.

Key words

In your personal file write down the following words and a one-sentence explanation for each:

Christian name

saint

Communion of Saints

patron saint